# The American Doctor

*An Autobiography*

Dr. Salvatore J. Forcina
M.D., F.A.C.S.

# The American Doctor

*An Autobiography*

GAUDIUM

# Gaudium Publishing

Las Vegas ◊ Chicago ◊ Palm Beach

Published in the United States of America by
Histria Books
7181 N. Hualapai Way, Ste. 130-86
Las Vegas, NV 89166 U.S.A
HistriaBooks.com

Gaudium Publishing is an imprint of Histria Books. Titles published under the imprints of Histria Books are distributed worldwide.

Library of Congress Control Number: 2023932289

ISBN 978-1-59211-209-8 (hardcover)
ISBN 978-1-59211-267-8 (eBook)

# Dedication

This book is dedicated to my beautiful and loving wife, with whom I have built a beautiful life.

My wish is that my granddaughter, Lennon, will read this book as a source of guidance. I wish for her to know that life will throw many things at her. The teenage years are difficult ones, and sometimes we make decisions we regret. This is part of life and growing up. I hope this book will serve as a guide for her.

I thank my parents for all they did, what they lived through, and the tremendous effort they gave each day. Despite the extreme circumstances, whether my parents were looking at the horizon to find the right way or looking for a sign of hope that tomorrow would be a better day, they always had their eyes looking up.

To my readers, thank you. Remember that no matter what, and no matter how difficult the path may be, you can and will succeed.

# Introduction

Throughout my life in the United States, I have had the opportunity to meet many people: from the most humble folk to professors and even some politicians. From each person I have met, I learned something I have continued to use in my own life. During many of these times and discussions about our respective lives and experiences, many of these people would tell me that what I have accomplished is great and that not too many people could have done or gone through what I did. I was often told I should write an inspirational book.

A friend of mine once told me you can't go through life without turning over any rocks. I have tried to leave my footprints to bring light and a path for life's dark times. In the process of writing this book, with the help of my wife and daughter, we shared some wonderful emotions and moments, reliving and recording various days and times. Although the cycle of life must continue, the reality is that time passes quickly. My father used to tell me this, but being young at the time, I didn't pay much attention to what he was saying. Nowadays, having matured and having limitations of my own, I understand more than ever what he was trying to tell me.

Although I have dabbled with the thought of writing a book for years, I never considered it seriously until my granddaughter, Lennon, was born. Lennon is a beautiful child, part of our lives, and because I don't know how long I will be able to help guide and talk to her, I want to be ever-present in her life through this book. I hope to inspire her and others, provide experience, help open peoples' eyes, and encourage them to make the right decisions in life. Although I used to have different hopes and dreams, these are my current ones.

Through time and experience, I have gained much wisdom. In today's brilliant, high-tech world, there are still many people around the globe who, sadly, will never reach their potential because of a lack of resources. Even more wrenching are those born into wealth or power that possess no ambition and simply waste their resources and opportunities. To some extent, a person is born into a life of predestination based on local and personal financial, medical and educational resources. It took a tremendous amount of energy, determination, dedication, and strength for me to confront my surroundings and shatter my own glass ceiling. I met my mentor late in life, decades after genuinely needing one, but it often made me think, *what if I had a mentor early on in my life?* Perhaps I could have shortened the many roads I traveled before realizing some were dead ends. It's easy to recognize a mistake once you've made it, but the more difficult thing is not to make that mistake again.

Originale, vissuto e proveniente del cuore (Original, lived, and coming from the heart). These are the personal experiences of my life. I have been honest and truthful, although some dates may be approximate. The details, however, are all accurate. I hope this book comforts readers looking for their dreams to come true. My path was twisted and windy. When you cross the ocean, it is essential to make it to the port on the other side. It is irrelevant whether you crossed in a rowboat or a mega yacht. If you reach your destination, you are already one of the lucky ones to make it and survive. The importance is to persevere. Never, ever give up. Avanti!

# Chapter 1
# Scauri

I write this book from the sunlit office of my residence in The Villages, Florida. My surroundings are comfortable, both emotionally and physically. I spend my days biking, golfing, and enjoying the fresh air outside. I am now a retired general and vascular surgeon, having been the Chief of Surgery at two North Jersey hospitals and having treated and operated on thousands of patients. I have been married to my bride, Roberta Petrillo, for forty-three years, and I am the father of one daughter and now a grandfather. My days as a seventy-nine-year-old retired doctor are very different from my earlier days and how my life began. This is the story of my life.

I was born in the Lazio region of Italy, in a small town called Scauri. Scauri is a coastal town south of Rome and north of Naples situated in the Gulf of Gaeta. The United States has a naval base in Gaeta; it's an elegant city with year-round tourists who enjoy its first-class restaurants and shop in its fashion boutiques. The famous Roman road, Via Appia, runs through Scauri. Scauri has a unique geographical location. It is protected from Siberian winds during the winter by the Aurunci mountains; thus, its temperature is mild, with the winter being short and pleasant. Scauri is well known among Europeans for its summer beaches. Some say Scauri was originally a Greek colony, Pirrea, and others say it is of Etruscan origin. Today, one can see the remains of the Cyclops Wall. This wall was constructed thousands of years ago by the ancestors of the Greeks and Etruscans. It is one of many artifacts in this region rich in history and cultural elements of many ancient civilizations.

This region also housed various influential leaders and famous people throughout time. For example, the Roman consul, Emilio Scauro, established his villa in Scauri. Close to Scauri is the city of Formia, where Cicero had his summer villa and where his tomb sits. Julius Caesar's friend, Planco, also had a residence in Gaeta. Just a few kilometers from Scauri is Minturno, the third Roman city. Minturno is located on the top of a mountain, and at its base is the Garigliano river, which ends up in the Mediterranean Sea. Around the year 800, the Saracen pirates, who kidnapped women and destroyed the city, invaded this area on numerous occasions. For protection, the people then decided to relocate their city to the top of the mountain in Minturno, using oxen to transport their belongings, and called their new city Traeto (from *trajinare*, which means drag). Throughout the centuries, this area was under many foreign dominations — the Spaniards in the fifteen hundreds and the French during the Napoleonic era; the Italian people were subjugated under foreign rule. Because of the injustices the Italian people suffered, some rebelled against the system, such as Michele Pezza, nicknamed Fra Diabolo. Fra Diabolo was a famous regional guerrilla leader who resisted the French occupation of Naples. Like a modern-day Robin Hood, he inspired the population to rebel against the oppressor.

Another town surrounding Scaui is the historical city of Capua. Capua is well known for its gladiator school from which another leader, Spartacus, came and fought the injustices of the Romans. In 73B.C., he fought against the Roman legion and was captured. Together with six thousand other warriors, he was crucified along the Appian Way, from Capua to Rome. This was to intimidate and warn those who tried to defy Roman law.

My paternal grandfather was from the city of Formia, Italy. Formia is a coastal summer resort, like Scauri, located approximately six kilometers down the road. Historically, Formia was where Marcus Tullius Cicero, a famous orator, lawyer, and philosopher, had a summer residence and where he died during the Roman civil war. Still today, many structures remain and are testimony to this glorious era. During my grandfather's time, the local people of Scauri were farmers. They worked the land and cared for some farm animals, such as cows or hogs, that provided milk, sausage, and prosciutto for the family. Lard was stored and saved and commonly used for cooking.

Life was very basic and routine. One woke up in the morning and had breakfast. What breakfast consisted of depended on the season. In the summer, for instance, when figs were abundant, a couple of figs with a slice of homemade bread or a piece of cheese were a common morning staple. Sausage produced from the animals and stored was taken to the fields for lunch. At noon, weather permitting, the workers used to gather under the shade of a tree and share what they each brought from home. The younger males were in charge of taking care of their family's resources, the animals, such as sheep, that they would take to the hills to graze. These young boys, known as shepherds, usually returned at sunset with an empty stomach, having had only a piece of hard bread and cheese all afternoon. The bread and cheese was made from their own prior hard work. The older males who worked the land would also return home at this time for a bowl of soup and wine made from local grapes. Usually, the women tended to the house and children while at the same time preparing meals for their families. Children shared the responsibility of daily life and contributed to the common good.

During winter days, many families would gather around the fireplace to keep warm. This was also where most meals were prepared. A metal tripod was placed on the ground with logs underneath and a caldron above. The meal generally consisted of items grown on the land, with a piece of pork added to give flavor and provide calories. The homes were made of stone, poorly ventilated, and cold, so between the cold and cooking, someone in the family had to tend to the fire and add logs. The soot from the constant fire would make everything black, and it was often the responsibility of the family's younger females to tend to such scrubbing with an old cloth and sand.

Communications were slow in arriving, and although there were some newspapers, most people were illiterate or had minimal reading skills, so sometimes, on a holiday or special occasion, if someone were able to read, everyone would gather around to hear what was happening in their local world. Because everyone contributed to the household's survival, it was commonplace for children to attend only a few grades of school; thus, there was a common resignation to the destiny of a very basic life. At that time, this made one inferior, and when such a person walked on the street, if a teacher, priest, or store owner passed by, that individual would remove his hat and lower his head to show deference and respect to *Il Signore*.

Holidays were very special mainly because of the distinction of the meals prepared. In these small towns, at that time, in some way or another, most people were related. The kitchen area was always the warmest in these homes because of the fire. Usually, this was where everyone stayed unless they were sleeping. Many individual families would gather in one kitchen, sharing the meals each family had prepared. The elders often gathered by the fireplace to smoke their pipes and share stories of the past or speak of their military service and what they had seen.

My grandfather, Nonno Salvatore, who I am named after, thought this life was static with no prospect of a better future. In the early 1900's he decided to emigrate to America. He had to leave his wife to care for their small children while trying to build a life for them in this new country. When he arrived in America, he accepted any job available. Sometimes he took jobs other people didn't want, such as mining. The kind of work environment offered poor ventilation, and often one's health suffered. His manual labor was poorly compensated at weeks' end. My grandfather and other immigrants were often exploited and taken advantage of mainly because of their poor grasp of the English language. I recall my father telling me stories of when Nonno worked on the railroad. After he and the other workers were paid, they used to walk to the barracks where they slept for the night. On more than one occasion, they were confronted by a group of delinquents waiting to beat them up and rob them. Nonno quickly wised up by sewing a pocket in the lining of his hat. On paydays, he hid his earnings in this hidden pocket in his hat and kept a few cents loose in his pocket. When approached, he would quickly throw the few loose coins onto the ground, diverting the thieves and secretly keeping the money he desperately needed to send back to his family in Italy. Every few months, those who could write would send a few lines to their family overseas. Those unable to write would ask a coworker or pay a service fee to have their letter written. With no other option, these individuals were at the mercy of the drafter's interpretation.

Nonno returned to Italy once or twice to visit his family and convinced his wife, Filipella (Filipa), to come with him to America. My grandmother's older, God-fearing relatives were superstitious and convinced her she would never see them again because the boat would sink. They changed her mind, and she never emigrated. After a few years, Nonno returned to Scauri, and with his savings from work in the United States, he was able to build a two-story home. The house was constructed of stone and without insulation. On the right side of the house was the kitchen and on the left was some sort of stable for the few animals they possessed and where they stored food and firewood. This was the typical style of house at the time, with access to the second-floor bedrooms by an outside ladder. We used to call this house in the mountain El Monte.

My parents were both born and raised in Scauri. As children, they attended school together, later dated, and were eventually married. It was common in those days to marry someone from the same town, as people didn't travel much nor had the means or opportunity to do so. Only the well-off and the educated traveled at this time because of the expense and lack of modern technology.

My mother was a simple lady, beautiful like every woman. She was born into a poor Italian family of six children (it is unknown whether one more may have been born and died during infancy) at the beginning of the nineteenth century. Like the youth of that time, she went to elementary school and studied the basics for two to three years, and because she was from a large, relatively poor family, she had to do chores around the house and help take care of the family's animals. They lived simply with big hearts and large sentiments. My mother often told me that her father, Giovanni, was a very humble, hard-working and peaceful man. Giovanni was a laborer and, with his carriage and horses, used to carry materials to make bricks and roof tiles to the only factory in Scauri, called La Ceramica Le Siece. One day, the horses slipped on wet asphalt. The carriage went backward into a stone wall, and its wheel became stuck. My grandfather got down from the carriage and pulled on the wheel. He was between the carriage and the wall, and when the horses could not proceed and backed up, the carriage crushed him. He lived for a few hours and left my mother and her brothers and sisters fatherless as young children.

My mother's family lived a few blocks from the famous Via Appia. Via Appia, built in 312 B.C., is a famous road known for its use by the Roman legions and other people, such as Mozart. This street is between the mountains and the shore; it was initially constructed because the Romans were involved in a war against the Samnite people and needed a route for people and goods. The Romans built monuments and buried their dead in tombs along the Appian Way, and many still exist today, although generally, they are in ruins. Over time, as the Roman Empire declined and the barbarians took over, there was no central authority, and the road condition deteriorated from lack of maintenance. In Scauri, over this period of neglect, the African winds blew sand over the streets and buried the road and nearby land parcels, preventing landowners from producing or collecting a harvest. This all changed after the end of World War I when a local politician was able to allocate funds to pave Via Appia, allowing the road to once again bring prosperity to the area by bringing cars, tourists, and various businesses as the transportation improved.

Since before Roman times, and well known for centuries, was a large area between Rome and Terracina (approximately thirty miles from Scauri) called the Pontine Marshes. The water from the mountains would collect and stagnate in the below-sea-level land, drawing many mosquitoes (anopheles labranchiae) that carried malaria. There had been many attempts at different times to drain this area, with only partial results. The real achievement was accomplished in the 1930s. My father and his friends were members of the team who worked on this site. My father used to tell me that he would get up at midnight on Sundays, and my grandmother would prepare a backpack for him with a few clothes and food for the entire week; the food primarily consisted of bread, cheeses, and sausages.

My father would meet a group of men, usually twenty other men from town, who gathered after midnight in the church parking lot during the wee hours of Monday mornings. They each road their bike, following the Appian Way towards Rome to arrive at the home base around 6-6:30 A.M. The home base was a previously-drained marsh where canals were built to prevent the accumulation of water. The home base had many tents where the men slept and ate for the week. Each day, the men had to continue another twenty-five to thirty kilometers to where they had to work and continue draining the marshes. At the high peak, more than twelve thousand people were working there. This went on for years. Eventually, with the arrival of DDT, they were able to exterminate the mosquitoes and, with them, the spread of malaria.

My father would return home on Saturdays at around 3 P.M. My grandmother would have hot water in a large container ready for him to clean himself. Once my father was clean and had changed his clothes, he would visit my mother since they were dating at the time. Whenever he was home, my father would help my mother's family with daily chores because her siblings were younger and, as you know, had lost their father. By Sunday afternoon, my father would need to rest because he would once again be starting the arduous journey back to work at midnight. Although this was a hard life, there were no other jobs. At the time, people like my father had little choice and resigned themselves to this life. With time, the land was drained and it became fertile for harvesting. Individual homes were built, and acreage was allocated for them to farm. People were young and risked their lives. Many of them ended up with malaria during this period. My father was lucky to have escaped this disease.

My father was also not formally educated. As a laborer, he had to rely on his hands and knowledge of building or fixing things to make a living and survive. He joined the Marine Corps of the Italian army as a young man, and when World War II broke out on September 1st, 1939, he was recalled into active duty. When I was born, my father was on the island of Rhodes; at that time, this island belonged to Italy. On the island of Rhodes, the Italians were under constant bombardment by the British ships, and there were many casualties. He was given leave for a few days to return to Italy and meet his infant son. After several days of arduous travel, my father arrived to meet me and visit my mother, only to return to the battlefront within twenty-four hours. I remember my father used to tell me of all the inconveniences he had to go through for him to come back, taking different trains, and because he was a Marine, he had to travel on a specific train. This particular train had left the station already, so he jumped onto the next train on which he was not permitted to ride. When the conductor came to ask for his ticket and saw he was on the wrong train, an argument ensued, and the conductor threatened to have my father arrested. When the police came aboard the train, my father was so desperate he said, "I am far away defending this country in war. Some members of my family are dead because of the war, and at this point, I do not care what you do to me, but before I die, I want to see my son."

During the war, the wintertime and life were very difficult. Lack of food, cold weather, and the absence of proper winter clothing made for much misery. This was the environment in which my parents lived. They saw many atrocities committed. Many people were killed and girls raped by the Allied Colony troops (French, Moroccan, Algerian, etc.) One can get a better idea of this if they watch the movie *Two Women* (*La Ciociara*), starring Sophia Loren. It references the alleged freedom given to Allied soldiers to have a free hand to steal, rape innocent girls and follow no laws. With this in mind and the fact that they were armed, there was no sense of justice, and poor people did not know where to seek help. Many young girls, after nine months, were forced to live with such consequences, bearing children of different or mixed races or colors. At that time in history and society, this was a stigma held against the mother and child, and they were relegated to effectively second-class citizenship. Consequently, it was challenging for that mother to have what was deemed a "proper" or "normal" family at the time.

My young mother was left to rear me on her own during a time of unrest and uncertainty in the country. Because of this, my father's sister, Giuseppina, brought my mother to El Monte to be with my father's family, who could help rear me. El Monte was the house on the hill I previously mentioned, and it showcased a beautiful panoramic view of the Gulf of Gaeta. As you know, sometime in the early nineteenth century, my paternal grandfather had built this house on adjoining parcels of property where members of the next generation, my father and his siblings, could all live. The families at that time had many members, usually around ten siblings. As these siblings grew up, married, and started their own families, their parents partitioned the land, allocating a portion of the property to each child. As the war progressed and the Italian government capitulated, many Italian soldiers returned to care for their families. Others were captured by the Germans and sent to Germany to work in factories due to the short supply of their own workers.

My father returned home. He was the head of his family at this time. The war had claimed his younger brother's life, and his father went unheard of for many months. The land in Scauri had been ravaged during the war by the constant bombardments. From the time my father returned to Scauri until the Germans left the area, he lived each day in constant fear of being captured. As such, groups of people, including my parents, had to travel back up into the mountains for protection.

Approximately thirty to forty kilometers from Scauri is the famous Abbey of Monte Cassino, strategically located on the top of a mountain and built around the year 500, although originally settled by the Volsci people around 500 B.C. It was later conquered by the Romans in 312 B.C. and given the name Cassino. Originally, a large temple was constructed at the top of the mountain and dedicated to the god Apollo. In the year 529, it was here that St. Benedict of Nursia established a monastery; it was the center of knowledge, and the Benedictine order created the first hospital in Europe. They also built a library with many manuscripts. The Benedictine rule was established at Monte Cassino and was later applied and followed by all other European monasteries.

Through the years, Cassino has suffered many attacks and much destruction, from the Lombards to the famous Battle of Monte Cassino in 1944, when the Allied forces bombarded the area and destroyed the monastery. The Germans were stationed on top of this mountain with their cannons, and with the view of the valley, they were able to prevent the advance of the Allied forces for many months, from December 1943 to June 1944. During this time, ninety-eight thousand Allied troops and sixty thousand Axis (Italian, German and Japanese) casualties occurred. There were many other civilian casualties from the bombs and land mines, and the constant bombardments killed many soldiers. The Italian word *"un cassino"* translates to "very bad" and is derived from this famous battle. There is also a famous Polish cemetery in the hills of Cassino in memory of the fifteen hundred Polish soldiers who lost their lives during this battle. After World War II, the abbey was completely reconstructed, taking into account its original model.

The Gustav Line was one of the defense lines created by the Germans to prevent the Allies from reaching Rome. This line went from the Mediterranean Sea to the Adriatic Sea; it cut Italy in two. In the north were the Germans, and in the south, the Allies. The neutral zone that went through Scauri was the partition between the Germans and the Allies. In between north and south Scauri, north of the River Garigliano is where the Germans planted thousands of mines underground. This neutral zone was no-mans-land, and the Germans told the population to flee. Unfortunately, many civilians still paid the consequences and lost their lives, and the area was completely destroyed. Because of all this, the remaining population collected the few items they possessed and escaped to the top of the mountains. Any other material things owned, they hid or buried.

Life in the mountains wasn't easy. Everyone lived in huts made of straw and had fires constantly burning for warmth. Severe lice infestations wreaked havoc. The absence of DDT or anything similar to kill bugs or lice required existing huts to be burned and new ones to be built every two weeks. My father, being used to manual work, was in charge of building and destroying the huts. Often the only warm clothes people had were old underclothes made of thick wool. The women would boil snow in a large cauldron to soak everyone's clothes and kill the lice. Other people in the mountains were not used to manual work because they were professors, etc., and were used to having other people do the manual work for them. Because these people generally lacked survival skills, they were the ones who usually found themselves in precarious positions, suffering the most and having the most casualties.

In the mountains, there were carob trees. Usually, this fruit is given to horses, but because of the lack of food, my family used to harvest the fruit, boil it, and make some kind of polenta. I remember later in life my father used to tell me this fruit can cause constipation. Perhaps because we were so young and hungry, my cousin and I would eat too much of it and often have abdominal cramps. My father had to dis-impact me on more than one occasion. As I mentioned, the weather was cold. My cousin and I were toddlers during this time and used to play and sit in the snow. Because we did not have appropriate clothing, we would get frostbite and cry. My grandmother used to warm a woolen cloth over the fire and put it on our backsides. That was the kind of medicine we had at that time.

Each day created a challenge. As a group, they had to travel to barter for goods and food to survive. During this time, money held no value; it was worth nothing. In complete desperation and fear, sometimes people would sneak down to the ocean to obtain salt from the seawater to be used as a bargaining chip for meager food rations.

My father often spoke of an incident where a group of women, including my mother, went from one valley to another to exchange a few things to get food for the family. Because of the cold weather and the paths they had to take, they found more than one dead German soldier. In desperation, they took the dead Germans' coats and boots. In the sky, Allied planes surveying the area noticed a group of people moving around wearing German uniforms and opened fire. Several people were killed. My father grabbed my mother, and they hid in a ditch. By some miracle, they survived and later escaped.

For my father's survival, he always put himself in-between women and disguised himself as a woman, too. During one such time, a group of Moroccan soldiers approached my family. My mother was very young and beautiful. One of the soldiers tried to grab her and take her away. My father jumped on the soldier and started a fight. Of course, the soldier had a gun and was ready to shoot my father on the spot. Only through the miracle of my grandmother's prayers and her kneeling in front of the soldier was my father's life spared. On yet another occasion, either having been tipped off or perhaps for some random reason, the German patrol going around the house in El Monte seemed to linger and wouldn't leave. My father, anticipating sometime like this might happen, had proactively put spikes inside the chimney of El Monte. It was, in fact, on this particular day that he had no choice but to hide inside the chimney. He quickly ascended the long spikes and silently waited in terror until the soldiers had left. My grandmother, nervous and desperate to save her son's life, went outside and offered the patrolling officers wine and sausages. She made sure they left half inebriated and happy to move along and leave her and her family alone.

As a young boy, I liked to be active, and I would say to my grandmother, "*Nonna... due Tedeschi...ci sono tre Tedeschi* (two Germans...there are three Germans)." I remember her grabbing me and taking me far away to prevent me from possibly giving away my father's presence. Their lives were in constant danger, and their survival instinct had developed to the highest level.

When the bombardments ceased after several months, people slowly came down from the mountains to return to the location of their homes and the ruins that were all that was left of them. Scauri also suffered under those bombardments, and its people paid the consequences in different forms. The atrocities of the war had killed members of certain families, and some had been crippled physically and psychologically. People had lost hope and were barely getting through each day. Many didn't know if dispersed relatives were alive or dead. Most of the homes in Scauri no longer had a roof, so people gathered under trees and made fires to protect themselves against the elements in the cold weather. The families gathered around the fires to warm up and cook meager meals as they consoled and comforted one another.

I recall my father telling me a story about one day a group of people was warming up near the fire; the light and flames must have been noticed by an Allied ship because a large bomb suddenly came from the sea, blasting and uprooting a large tree that killed several people and injured many others. A bomb fragment had scratched my forehead while my mother was holding me. Because the skin of that area is thin, there was a lot of blood, and in my mother's desperation for her young child's injury, she did not realize that she had suffered a much worse bleeding, gaping wound on her leg. I recall that for her entire life, she had a deformity in that area. She suffered the consequences of that wound for many months, and most probably, because of the lack of antibiotics and appropriate medical care, she developed an infection of the bone. Years later, the bone had to be scraped and debrided. As a doctor, so many years later, thinking of the possible consequences of that type of wound, I realize she could have died. That bomb uprooted a large tree and created a large crater. I try to imagine people desperately running in different directions, seeing some of their relatives dead, others bleeding, and there was no one to help them. Combine this with their hunger, no shelter, lack of proper clothing, and the cold weather — the conditions were miserable. The only things they had for consolation were each other and their prayers to God.

When and if German soldiers were seen, someone would signal either by whistling, yelling, etc. and when this happened, my father used to escape to a hidden area formed by rocks and bushes along the edge of the creek dividing their property from the next one. One day my father and his family were preparing the soil for plantings so that food could once again be harvested. Some women sounded the alarm, signaling a German patrol was near. My father, to save his life, had to run and jump into the creek and hide under the bushes at the edge. The bushes had thorns, and he sustained many scratches and cuts. I recall my father telling me the water was ice cold because it came from the top of the mountain, and he became numb. The Germans continued to advance and, with their bayonets, were poking into the area around the creek. My father had to wait, bearing hypothermia, and by some miracle, he was not discovered that day.

Another time when my father was working in the fields, a patrol once again was seen advancing. My father ran, trying to cross the street for protection; however, he noticed another German patrol was further up the street he was planning to cross. An old lady noticed my father was in trouble. She told him to get to her side where the Germans would not see him, and they crossed the street together. My father reached a gate that he could climb over, but in desperation, while climbing over the spikes on top of the gate, he slipped, and part of his clothes got stuck on the points, leaving him suspended in the air. He could have been discovered at any time and would have been shot. Again, this lady saw his predicament. She put her body against the gate and offered her head so he could step and lift himself up and over the spikes. He escaped. My father used to explain how many people suffered and were angry and afraid. Many of them had also lost loved ones and were, therefore, resigned to keep fighting and helping each other.

When the Allied troops crossed the Garigliano River and the German soldiers retreated through Rome, people were hungry, and with the spring approaching, those that owned land were in a hurry to clean the property and start planting seeds. Although the Allied forces had begun removing land mines from the area, this took a long time and required a lot of effort. Many private citizens took this risk upon themselves. Some suffered the consequences. One day my father was going back to work at the ceramic factory and saw our distant cousin working on his land. After saying hello, my father inquired what he was doing and was told he was clearing the land. My father urged him not to because of the unpredictable landmines in that area, but our cousin insisted, saying he was nearly done and had only a small piece of land left to finish. My father said goodbye and left, proceeding on his way to work. Incredulously, he was not more than one block away when he heard a loud blast and right away realized it was his cousin. Desperation can make people do irrational things, and a wrong decision like this one sadly had fatal consequences. Many years later, when I returned to Italy, I met this cousin's widow, who was a very nice lady and invited me to her home for dinner.

# Chapter 2
# Azul

The war destroyed everything: people's homes, lives, and sometimes their families. It also broke many people's spirits. There was tremendous physical devastation to fields, and jobs were hard to come by. Little or nothing was known about Post Traumatic Stress Syndrome in those days, so often, returning soldiers and their families were left to simply deal with it and move on.

The factory my father had once worked for was expanding and opening a new factory in a province of Buenos Aires, in a city named Azul, in Argentina. Life was not so stressful in Argentina; food was abundant, and the risk of war was remote. My father, traumatized from the war, wanting to be as physically far away as possible from the horrible memories, and being offered a new job in a new place, with his transatlantic passage paid for, took the opportunity and ran. About fifty other men from the factory with various skill sets, such as carpenters and masons, were also offered such an opportunity. They each had a two-year contract with repatriation guaranteed if so desired.

Some of these men had attended a university in Italy for a year to two but never finished. Because Italy was more advanced than Argentina at the time, some of these men went to Argentina with a feeling of superiority or a sense of ego. They felt their skill sets were superior to most Argentinian people at that time who used creativity and their hands to produce any work product. At times, these egos or men's feelings of trying to exert themselves above their colleagues caused animosity, jealousy, or isolation even within members of extended families. For instance, some men threw parties or gave gifts to try to ingratiate themselves to a boss in the hope of getting a superior work position and thus earning more money. In reality, however, all of these workers came from a desperate place with limitations, so they were forced to do anything to survive and by any means. Sadly the fight to survive can create a dark world. Some tried to deceive others by pretending to be something they were not; some showed indifference in return, while others accepted it at face value. While some of these problems were temporary, others extended to the following generation. Regardless of the timing, this obviously created a lot of friction.

Today Azul is a city of approximately fifty-five thousand people and approximately three hundred kilometers from Buenos Aires. The land is flat, and due to its rich topsoil, it is an excellent place to grow wheat, corn, and alfalfa. The land is also well known for breeding cows, sheep, and pigs. The animals were left to graze freely due to the mild temperatures, and there wasn't a need for stables. At the beginning of the century, windmills were installed to allow water to flow and feed the animals. The owners of such parcels of land were called Estancieros. An Estanciero could own thousands of acres of land and hundreds of livestock or pigs, etc. Most Estancieros were well off and well known at the time, and their names held prestige. They had major influence over regional political decisions. However, it was not always like this.

At the end of the eighteen hundreds, the land of the later Estancieros was dominated by Indians. There were few, if any, such settlements because the Indians constantly attacked the settlements: causing destruction and rape, and animals were often stolen.  In order to encourage further settlements south of the city, the government at that time encouraged people to resist and push back the Indians and their attacks by offering free parcels of land. The sole requirement to obtain a parcel of land was to have enough pesos to buy the barbed wire from England (few were able to do so) to enclose the land's perimeter. If you could afford to do this, one could claim thousands of acres of land this way.

The people who worked the land and took care of the animals were called gauchos. They were simple people of good nature but generally illiterate. From generation to generation, they lived on these farms and occasionally were able to go to a nearby town and purchase some clothes. Unfortunately, some of the gauchos were abused by the property owners, while some of the female children ended up as household servants in the homes of the landowners in the city of Azul; this was the best-case scenario a child in these circumstances could have for their future.

After the war, during the Peron regime, Argentina was able to sell its different farm products to Europe. As a result of the two World Wars, Europe became a huge consumer of Argentina's produce. Europe's industries and food production were decimated, and its people were starving. Argentina was lucky enough to be able to provide the necessities Europe needed. As such, Argentinian exports to Europe of grains and meat to feed the starving populations increased tremendously. The benefits of these exports made Argentina richer; thus, the land was more valuable. President Peron was Argentina's attaché in the pre-war era and had been in Rome during the time of Mussolini. It was there he learned from the master politician, Mussolini, and when he returned to Argentina, he implemented those ideas with phenomenal success. As such, he was later elected to be the supreme leader of Argentina for years.

My father left for Argentina in 1947, leaving my mother and me behind. She was young and now a mother of two young sons. My father, thinking we could have a better and easier family life, sent for us, and we arrived in Argentina in May of 1949. I had turned eight one month before, and my brother was about eighteen months old. It wasn't an easy task to leave our family, friends, and country behind. We brought our customs and thoughts with us, as all people do. Although Christopher Columbus was Italian, it was a Spanish monarch who contracted him and subsidized his expedition. Along with Spanish colonization everywhere from Mexico south, except for Brazil, Argentina had the culture, language, and customs of the Spanish motherland. As such, upon our arrival to the city of Azul, we realized everything was new to us: people expressing themselves in an unfamiliar language, people with different customs, way of dress, and a new and different cuisine.

My parents rented a room with a separate kitchen in the home of an older Italian couple that had also emigrated from Italy to Argentina about fifty years prior. The gentleman of the house had a *carezze* (cart) with a horse. This was the ancestor of the taxi. Taxies were few and unaffordable for a regular person at that time. The gentleman and others like him made their living and spent most of their day waiting by the train station for potential passengers.

The house was on the outskirts of town, a typical colonial style with two or three basic adjacent rooms facing an open patio protected from the sun or rain by an extending roof. These homes were very simple, with a brick wall five or six feet in height surrounding the house, and a wooden gate at the entrance offered access to the house with a front garden to walk through. The house had little insulation and a metallic zinc roof causing loud noise during rainstorms and extremes of temperature during different seasons. Between the roof and ceiling was a large area without insulation. During hot months the trapped air made our sleeping room as hot as an oven, and during the cold months, it was the exact opposite. The house didn't have any screens, so if you chose to open a window, you had to deal with any outside noise and mosquitos.

We were located one block from the railroad, and although pedestrian traffic was allowed, there was no car traffic or vehicular access. Whenever it rained, this isolated dirt road got muddy and became flooded. In a very short time, however, I hung around with other children, and we played in the street, not minding the dust or lack of asphalt. While my father was away working all day, my mother was left to care for my brother and me. We were two young boys in a small space. There was a lot of pressure to keep my young brother and me quiet, which put a lot of extra stress and worry on my mother, particularly after one evening when the gentleman of the house told my father he should have better control of us. My father, traumatized by the war, really amped up his pressure to be extra quiet and respectful of the home's owners after that day.

Almost adjacent to the kitchen was a corral for the gentleman's horse, with a small storage shed. The corral floor was dirt and partially covered by the same zinc roof as the house. The horse spent the night there to protect itself from the harsh weather. However, when it rained, the corral floor became muddy and slippery. Whether wet or dry, there was a constant smell of the horses' feces. Wet floors were a common issue. Across from the open patio was a small house my mother used as a kitchen. When it rained, the patio tile would be wet and slippery, and because my mother had to go back and forth to check on the food, as she was always doing other things at the same time, one day, she slipped and had a bad fall.

There was little technology. My mother, not yet speaking any Spanish, and being a new immigrant in a foreign country far from her homeland and family, felt very isolated. All my mother had in any form of communication with her family was through the very slow international mail. Often, when I would play in the street with other local children, my mom would come to check on me and ask if the mail for that day had come. I was too young to understand the meaning behind that question, but now, I understand that my mother, in her solitude, was anxious to receive news from her family back in Italy. I can still remember her resignation whenever I said there was no mail and her hope for a letter to come the next day.

On those days when my mother did receive a letter, especially from her sister-in-law, with whom she was very close, she would read and reread that letter almost as though she had missed something the first time around. I wish I had been an artist to capture those moments because, for my mother, those moments were so special to her. In her inner, private world, those letters produced so much joy and held such value to and for her. My father tried to help my mother through these initial moments of isolation by reminding her of all the things they had already gone through during the war, how they had survived and had each other and their lives.

I remember the first few months of life in Argentina being filled with extreme discipline and the constant advice of my parents to behave myself and stay out of trouble. My father was greatly affected by any complaints about my behavior or me. After the school day was over, I would spend most afternoons playing with other children in the street, either running around or kicking an improvised ball made of rolled socks stuffed with newspaper. Sadly, because of our ball's poor construction, it would lose shape and shred into pieces after many kicks. Nonetheless, it provided hours of entertainment.

Although my family wasn't fortunate enough to have a radio in the early 1950s, a friend of mine, also from an Italian family, happened to have one. So, every weekday, Monday through Friday at 6 PM, when the factory alarm's sounded signaling the end of the work day, like the gratification of a dog trained with Pavlov's reflex, I would show up at his house. Together we would press our ears close to the radio to hear the broadcast of Tarzan, and for those thirty minutes, we were transported to a fantasy land of adventure otherwise unknown to us.

Between my mother's feelings of isolation, my father working, and remaining traumatized from the war, the future was very uncertain. On more than one occasion, I witnessed hidden tears wetting my mother's face, and I remember when, to vent her frustrations, she used to say to me, "*Figlio siamo venuti a questa terra sbagliata*" (we have come to the wrong place). Still, today, after so many years, those memories are so vivid, and I always used to wonder how my parents kept pressing on without going insane.

As in almost all cultures, future generations generally inherit the customs of the preceding generations and are brought up in a similar fashion. My parents' ancestors carried traditions of being independent and working to preserve the land, growing tomatoes to make different kinds of sauce to cook pasta and meat or fish. In the early days, when one owned a pig and the time came to kill it, sausages, prosciutto, and other such meats were made.

My father used to buy sardines at the local fish store. He would very carefully clean and cure them, placing them in jars to be consumed when needed. Olives, green beans, eggplant, and other similar vegetables were prepared and stored in the same fashion. I recall some of my local friends being delighted when they joined us for dinner; they were amazed by how simple and delicious basic vegetables and other such things were because they were prepared in ways they were not accustomed to.

Growing up, Sundays were special days. Starting in the early morning, my mother would gather the ingredients needed to make pasta sauce, and sometimes, she would make fresh spaghetti (at other times, she would use previously made pasta ). Then, my mother would cover her long, beautiful hair with a handkerchief and start the tedious process of making the sauce. Using a ceramic container and placing the ingredients inside, she would carefully cook the sauce over a *fuoco lento* (a very low flame) while gently stirring everything with a wooden spoon. This process took hours to complete, and in the interim, she would tend to other household chores such as laundry, etc.

Little by little, the kitchen and other rooms became impregnated with the sweet aroma of the sauce, stimulating my appetite. My mother always took pride in her cooking and would return every few minutes to stir the sauce, have a look and make sure it wasn't cooking too fast or burning. As a young boy with limited self-control and generally being hungry, without raising any suspicion and when my mother was occupied in another room, I used to sneak into the kitchen and slowly lift the cover of the pan and dip a piece of bread in the sweet nectar my mother had made. Very quietly, I would find a secret corner of the house to slowly consume this forbidden treat. To combat any evaporation as the sauce cooked, a small amount of water was added so that the sauce became thick and pasty. Sometimes my mother would taste the sauce and, being proud of her work; she used to say, *"E propio buona questa salsa!"* (this sauce is very good!). Sometimes she used to be surprised that the level within the pot was so low and sometimes would say she must have miscalculated her measurements, but I think she knew of my sin and, like the good mother she was, always forgave my transgressions.

In these early times of my youth, as the holidays were approaching, my mother would make the feast more significant by baking a cake. For my brother and me, the sweet smell from the kitchen was a powerful stimulus for our senses. Once the cake was completed, my mother used to admonish us not to touch or taste it as it was to be saved for the special day, Easter Sunday. Sometimes this warning proved not enough, so from then on, she used to deter us from our temptations by telling us there was a snake inside the cake and only after the blessing on Easter Sunday would this snake disappear. Being young and naive, we believed her. I know my dear mother would have given us anything to see us happy, but because of our financial limitations and to safeguard the cake, a real treasure in our home, reserved only for very special occasions, she had to trick us. Those days were very different and special as such things were not common in our home. I can tell you, however, that during those years, my brother and I wished so much those damned snakes weren't in our cake!

One day, shortly after arriving in Azul, I was playing with some kids in the street. One kid brought along some rotten eggs, and we thought it would be funny to throw them against the gate of a house near an abandoned piece of land close to the railroad. We all did this, but I guess I was the only child recognized, and someone complained to my father. I received severe corporal punishment, and with a bucket of water, I had to clean the mess of dried and broken eggs and the flies feeding off such a rotten and foul-smelling meal. I learned a lesson, and this incident left a mark that has stayed with me.

These were the special times of my youth. My life was simple. I remember being young and hearing my father discuss what he had left behind and feeling nostalgic about his family and place of birth. As a grown man, in a similar fashion, my father would ask me, "Salvatore, do you remember when you were young, and you used to ask me, "*Papà, quando e Domenica?*" (Dad, when is Sunday?) Being young, poor, and not yet knowing the days of the week, I was anxious for the day when my mom would cook meat. This was a luxury reserved for this one special day of the week.

Despite our economic circumstances, I was fortunate to always receive the affection of my parents who cared, and lived in a household in which examples were set. I have come to miss those days as I have gotten older. I think the idea of Sunday being a special day has been repeated in many Italian families, and perhaps, whoever is reading this may also recall the days when their family all got together around the table: older and younger family members, visitors, and extended family all admiring and toasting the elder person of the house who lifted their glass to say, "*Alla salute!*"

Looking back at those days now, I realize the focal point of my childhood was to avoid conflict or be in trouble with my father. Although the images of war would never leave my father and had scarred him, I was an innocent child of a family lucky to have survived the atrocities of war. Those images sadly became his guide for life, and the reality of this affected us as children, particularly me, as I was the older child and my brother was still very young. My family had been blown about like seeds in the wind, and there was no security in our destiny. I was at the mercy of the wind, not knowing which direction I was going. Today, recalling those days, I can't understand how I was able to survive and find the right path in the labyrinth of my life. There was never an obvious exit door at any moment.

In Argentina at that time, a few days before Christmas, the government gifted to its entire population a pan dulce, which in Italy is called a panettone, and a bottle of cider. In Latin countries, the feast of the Epiphany is celebrated on the sixth day of January. It is also on this day when children receive their presents, etc. On many occasions, at some of the public buildings, free gifts were distributed to children. Because of some of our previous indiscretions and also in part because of some sort of isolation, my brother and I were never told or heard about these gifts. I remember on that day, *El dia de Los Reyes*, the day of the Three Kings, I saw children playing in the streets with so many toys. They had received them for free, but in my mind, it was because their parents could afford such toys, compared to my parents, who could not. I was never made aware that such free things existed. I never felt included or part of that group of kids. It was very sad to think that already, at such a tender age, we were deceived, as our neighbors never thought to tell my parents so we could share in this too. Perhaps because of mankind's primitive instinct to survive, people kept such secrets to themselves so their own children could benefit, and the government's supplies would not run out if too many people learned of this "secret."

These are the things I remember most vividly, and now, as I have gone through so many of my own struggles, everything has a different meaning to me. I appreciate even more the endurance of my family and the hardships they suffered to survive. My parents tried hard to instill in me the virtues necessary for survival, not be intimidated, and work very hard if I wanted to succeed in life. One of my blessings was having such parents; I will never forget them. The little things they could give me materialistically were no comparison to the larger lessons of life they passed on.

What I know today is not to allow such circumstances to make you endlessly cry or constantly live in self-pity. One must face the adversity of the present and act so the future will improve. As in quicksand, you must be careful of your movements, calculating which ones give you the best chance for escape and survival. Because all the time, I had a goal, and even though I didn't know how, I didn't lose hope. I dreamed that one day I would find the right path behind the mountain blocking my view. The desire to find a new way to circumvent the obstacle(s) was with me all the time because I was aware that if I gave up, all was lost. This was not my nature. The determination to survive was instilled in me by example each day as my parents persevered through life. This is not something you can learn from books but solely through the experiences of the big book of our lives.

# Chapter 3
# Conversations with My Father

When I was young, and during the summer evenings, we ate dinner in our backyard in Argentina. There was a patio adjacent to our kitchen. As you exited the kitchen door, down two or three steps, on the right side was our water pump (at that time, we did not have a connection to the city water supply). The patio was partially covered with a cement structure, and to its left, an "L" shape followed, covering a long outside corridor that continued to the front of the house. The patio floor was discarded ceramic tiles from the factory where my father worked. He obtained them at a very reasonable price because they were deformed in some way and therefore of no use to the company. Like most Spanish colonial houses, a pergola protected the patio from bright light and provided a good home for grapes to grow and make our own wine.

This was the place where our family discussions usually took place. The patio was my family's private place, and my mother, following her Italian roots, always prepared well-balanced meals, healthy and delicious, no matter how simple. Although there is and always was a lot of meat consumption in Argentina, at my parents' home, the main dishes were made from products cultivated in our garden. We did not consume much red meat, but my mother would often bake rabbit (from our yard) in the oven along with golden potatoes. We would have fresh salad mixed with radishes or products my father had previously jarred, such as sardines or eggplants.

One of my favorite meals my mother prepared was gnocchi. Her gnocchi were very light, made from potatoes and covered with a sweet marinara sauce. A nice sprinkling of Parmesan cheese coated the gnocchi and my plate, enhancing the flavor. There was always a bottle of wine on the table during our meals, which was for all of us to enjoy and was not a mystery or something kept away from us. At the time, I used to mix my wine with water to dilute it, but I never lost control or saw my parents abuse alcohol. My parents also kept liquor in the house, which was reserved for guests and visitors. In general, either at noon or dinner time, we all gathered together around the table because this was our epicenter. Here the past was present, and future dreams were born. My mother used to add her religious upbringing to the mix and tell me, "*Figlio, dici sempre se Dio vuole*" (Son, if God wishes).

Like most Italian families past and some present, on Sundays around noon, my family would enjoy a nice meal together. It was an elaborate meal and certainly not a daily occurrence. My father would spend those Sunday mornings planting, harvesting, and transplanting things in his garden. As he toiled the hours away, my father, being happy, used to sing popular songs in Italian, known to him from his youth. We would have antipasto, followed by a small pasta dish, followed by secondi, or second and the main course. Salad or fruit followed the second course. For an Italian mother like mine, this was all very special because Sunday was different than the other days of the week. To her, the act of preparing a meal was an art and a passion; the dominical event of all of us seated together around the table sharing our special meal. My mother used to decorate the table with flowered tablecloths, and the dishes would embrace each other: a flat dish for the antipasto and a deeper dish for the secondi.

As mealtime approached, my mother, knowing my father would want to finish whatever he was working on, would call him to ask, "*Armando, che dici? La butto la pasta?*" (Armando, what do you say? Can I boil the pasta?) For any of my readers unfamiliar with the pasta business, the timing of the pasta is critical because most Italians like their pasta al dente, and the pasta must not be over or undercooked; it must be just right. This precise moment of cooking the pasta to perfection is a very short window of time. Because of this concern, if my mother didn't see my father coming, she would remind him to hurry up. "*Armando, vieni che la pasta si fa fredda!*"

(Armando, come to eat before the pasta becomes cold!) He would answer, *"Vengo...vengo subito!"* (I'm coming right away!) By the time my father stopped what he was doing, washed his hands, and sat down to join us, now all seated together, I could sense my mother's apprehension. Whenever my father finished his dish, my mother would ask, *"Come e' stata la pasta?"* (How was the pasta?) My father then used to say, *"E' stata speciale."* (It was special.) Between some glasses of wine and our delicious meal, our worries were nonexistent for a while.

Sometimes my father would reminisce about his days as a young Marine in the Italian army. He would tell me what went on while he was stationed on the island of Rhodes. The nights were cold, and they were under constant bombardment from the British fleet that was not too far away. The men at that time wore heavy coats made of wool. The proximity of the Mediterranean waters created an ever-present midst that would, over the hours, saturate the wool fabric, making it heavy and uncomfortable. My father said he used to walk back and forth to keep from falling asleep while on duty. He even used to carry a handkerchief to dip into the ice-cold water of the small creeks formed by falling water from the tops of the mountains and place it around his neck in the hope that the discomfort would help keep him alert for the remainder of his shift. When such measures didn't work, so as not to fall asleep and potentially be court-martialed, he would go to a nearby tree, remove his metal helmet and bang his head against the tree to awaken himself.

Finally, at midnight, when his guarding duties ended, he would fall asleep, only to be roused by the sound of the siren alarm and wake in the midst of panic and confusion as everyone attempted to deal with and prepare for the incoming bombs. This went on for weeks, and he said he was exhausted and always dreaded when the next day arrived and it was time to return to duty again. He didn't know how he could face it again or any longer.

My father was a serious man who had, and instilled a lot of discipline. I genuinely believe his life was forever altered by the war. He saw many men, including his younger brother and brother-in-law, killed. The few possessions he accumulated from saving money since working as a boy were also lost or destroyed. He knew his father despaired for months without knowledge of his existence, whether he was alive or dead or captured and forced into manual labor by the Germans. Because he wasn't able to receive a formal education, he was self-taught and became a voracious reader. Looking back now, as an older man myself, I wonder what could have been if he had had different opportunities. Sadly, the war seemed to harden my father's attitude and adherence evermore to a methodical life. He seldom trusted anyone and had phobias about future wars.

I remember that while we ate, my father would at the same time irrigate the vegetables in our garden that he used to cultivate and sell for extra income. He had a regular job during the day, and at night when he used to return, he took his bicycle which had a small box with two wheels attached to the back and would fill this box with the vegetables he grew and bring them to his clients. On those calm, serene nights filled with stars, I used to listen to my father recount his experiences as a boy. When he was fifteen or sixteen and living in Italy, he used to help the family by rotating the dirt in the ground, seeding the area, and planting vegetables. In those times, the chances of people achieving their aspirations were almost impossible. The desire to succeed in life, accomplish their goals, and improve their children's lives was only a dream. It seemed their life was predestined, and their destiny was set and determined ahead of time. When my father was tilling the ground, he unearthed some roots that could be used as food for the animals, especially horses. In those times, horses were the means of transportation for the delivery of merchandise because the automobile was in its infancy. I recall he used to explain that he made bundles of these roots (couch grass or weeds), and at the end of the day, he used to stand on the side of the road where the horse carriages passed. For a few cents, he would sell these roots to the drivers. With the few pennies he made and saved, as time passed, he saved enough to buy himself a bicycle of which he was very proud. Unfortunately, his happiness did not last long because, after a while, someone stole his bike. I remember the expression on his face when recounting this story, as he still felt the sense of loss and invasion. For him, it seemed he was always reliving these moments.

We often listened to the radio, our only form of technology in Argentina. There was an Italian station we liked that played old Italian songs. Most of them were very sentimental, describing the condition of the people, their migration to other countries, and leaving the Port of Naples with the hope of improving their lives and the dream of a better future. One of the songs was called "*Partono I Bastimenti per Terra assai Lontana*" (The ships are leaving for a far away land). Other songs were romantic, like those that expressed the love for one's mother. The song was called "*Mamma son tanto felice.*" I recall most of the songs being sung by Carlo Butti. There were operatic arias, like from the *Barber of Seville*. I was not used to listening to such music, but between its repetition and my father's limited knowledge of the background and stories of the operas, I grew curious to learn. So, little by little, in my own way, I grabbed any opportunity to improve my understanding and knowledge of opera and the classics. The desire for this knowledge has continued to increase throughout my entire life. To this day, it continues to provide me with happiness, and each day, even a sad day, is made better when I hear such music. The notes are soothing to my soul.

The radio we had was primitive, and because of this, it would react to weather miles away. There was static of epic proportions. There was a station that broadcast classical music, and I used to listen to this whenever I could. I remember one day when I was sick in bed; I was able to listen to the opera *Il Matrimonio Secreto* by Cimarosa. This was the first time I was able to listen to an entire opera. Despite the inconvenience of the static and poor quality of sound, the music opened my eyes and motivated me to read and study the true meaning behind each opera I would eventually have the joy of hearing. Through those years, I became self-educated. This knowledge showed me the world in a different way compared to the world of my parents, who were not fortunate to receive even the few small opportunities I had then. Because of this, their knowledge was even more limited and very basic.

When I was a student at the Universidad de La Plata (in my twenties), there was a theater, and for a few pesos, I used to buy a ticket to the opera that gave me access to a seat at the highest point of the theater. While sitting up there, I could spot the empty seats on the main level. Therefore, during intermission, I quickly went down and took one of those seats where I could truly enjoy the performance. Unfortunately, not too many people would go to see these performances, and because of that, the theater shut down. It was one of the few pleasures and indulgences I had at the time.

During this time, I also began to like ancient history: the stories of how people used to live and what their customs were. The arias and melodies of the music I listened to paralleled the narrative as they sang about peoples' lives and their ambitions and desires for a better future. When I was a teenager attending school, some of the other students found out I had an inclination toward opera and its musicality. Because of their poor knowledge or limited experience, they used to tease and mock me in front of others. Of course, sometimes I did not take this very well, but because I was alone, I had to lower my head, keep quiet and move on. As time passed, and even to this day, I find it difficult to find and talk to others who truly understand and appreciate this type of music.

During my father's youth, possessing a radio was a major event. For the first time, one could receive information about the events of the world. The working people at this time would get up early in the morning to go to work when it was dark, and after many hours of work, would return to their families when it was dark again. One can only imagine what kind of life they had in the wintertime when it was cold and rainy. To many people, life was very simple, and my parents, grandparents, and great-grandparents all continued a cycle of life in which there was no difference from one generation to another. There was a sense of common misery; everyone seemed resigned to accepting this as what "normal" was. The radio began to alleviate this loneliness by giving people something to look forward to, listen to, and hear about.

An important event of my father's youth was a religious celebration in the square across from the church in their town. At the time, the youth or teenagers would put on their best clothes, congregate in the square, and the boys and girls would socialize and enjoy the available local food. Sometimes the town would hire a band of musicians to play selections from various operas. This was major entertainment for the townspeople as these events were rare and treasured because of the poverty, and such days were special and unique. Through these stories and because I was slowly becoming an older child, I began to admire my father very much, and these stories started to become and continue to remain important to me.

# Chapter 4
## Casita

After my parents, my brother, and I had been living in Argentina for a while, between 1950-1951, my dad was able to acquire a small, inexpensive piece of land to build a home on for our family. This land parcel was outside the city, a few blocks from where the elderly couple who originally functioned as our landlords lived and situated between two factories: Ceramica, where my father worked, and the other called Curtiembre (cowhide). The hides were treated using different chemicals that drained into a ditch running alongside the dirty street. In the summer, a foul smell filled the air, and eventually, after many years of polluting the area and the water becoming contaminated, the factory had to close. In those days, people were unaware of or unconcerned with environmental issues. Everyone was just living a basic life and trying to survive. This all changed when the new generation became largely literate. With the improvement of communication, many began to ask questions, but this all came about years after we moved away from the area.

While my father was at work all day at the ceramic factory, my mother would prepare all the bricks for our house and have the mortar mixed and ready. Then, after my father returned from work at night, we would go over to this piece of land, turn on a single light bulb and start building, brick by brick, wall by wall. I recall doing this during the winter because the darkness came early. My father used to plug in an extension cord so he could use all the mortar my mother had prepared; he would leave nothing to waste. Finally, after some time, two rooms were finished, and we were able to move in. There was still no kitchen, so my mother used to prepare our meals outside in a small hut, which was dark with only a small window and no ventilation. Although the hut was a temporary thing, those days were hard.

My father was happy with the location of our home because of the proximity to his job. Our parcel of land was an abandoned place, full of high grass, and the earth had not been tilled for years. The roots of the wild grass penetrated deep into the earth, requiring long hours of digging with a pick to create an opening so they could be pulled out. My poor mother took this job upon herself while my father worked his regular job during the day. If I close my eyes, I can still remember and picture that poor soul doing such hard work, getting blisters and calluses on her gentle hands.

It took many years to finish the construction of the house because my father, having lost everything once before during the war, was terrified to have it happen again, therefore would only buy materials, such as one window at a time, when he could pay in cash. He could never make himself comfortable with the idea of taking a loan because of the trauma and years of uncertainty inflicted upon him by the war.

During the course of building this home and working at the ceramic factory, my father became very ill. He went to many doctors who each prescribed antibiotics on more than one occasion. Because of my present knowledge as a physician, I know those antibiotics produced pseudomembranous enterocolitis (an injury to the lining of the intestine, which as a consequence, affects the absorption of food. This then causes diarrhea and weakness). This illness was very disabling for my father because of his constant loss of electrolytes, but my father had to continue working because of our economic situation. His diet consisted of rice and toasted bread, while for liquid, my mother gave him the remaining water used to boil the rice he ate. This went on for several years. He was weak, and we all strained to help as much as we could. In reality, my mother was drained, caring for two young children, and we were simply children, capable of only so much.

I recall, on more than one occasion, as the years passed and I grew older, that some Italian contemporaries and their families paid visits to my father during this time. These visitors often suggested that I go to work at the factory where my father worked so I could further help out my parents while discouraging the idea of advancing my studies into a career. Some couldn't see past the immediacy of helping my father financially in the short term, and some were jealous that I would have a different future than them. Some had narrow minds based on society at the time. My father felt strongly about me having a formal education, however, because he did not have the chance to study, and if I wanted to study, he would do anything to make that possible, even if he had to sell the unfinished house he was building.

In life, the desperate need for survival will either kill or motivate people to do incredible things. Today, we call those motivated by such circumstances champions. However, in those days and in that environment, after coming from the war in Europe, people didn't question things as much, and when someone got sick, there was a very simple answer; such as he was old, or it was his destiny, and if somebody was a religious person it was said that it was the will of God. In doing what they did, I feel that my parents are the heroes of this world for whom, in my imagination, I have built an eternal statue on top of the highest mountain. The lessons I have learned from my parents, things communicated to me without even the articulation of a word, became the fire inside me to always keep going. My parents' experiences gave me the tenacity to fight, work hard, persist, and never give up. Any success I have achieved in my life, I owe to them. To me, all their actions and adventures reaffirm every day of my life, more and more, the desire to succeed. Therefore, I applied myself to studying without a break. In doing so, I knew I would make my parents proud, and all their sacrifices would not have been in vain.

I recall one day, my father was going to repair a leak he noticed in the roof of our house. He bought a container of solid asphalt, and this asphalt needed to be heated to melt into its liquid form. My father placed the container over the stove and used a stick to stir it every once in a while. Slowly, the wet liquid tar was becoming soft and very hot, and at one point, it got so hot the container caught on fire inside the kitchen. My father grabbed the handle and ran outside onto the patio, where he dropped the container. He was badly burned and suffered tremendous pain on his entire left arm and the upper left part of his chest. Lots of blisters and exposed skin followed, and he had some very bad days. My mother would have to change the dressing daily as the burn had to be covered; you could see this was torture for him. Despite everything, he went to work every day. His job at that time was to load bricks onto big trucks. The bricks, after being cooked at a high temperature, had a residual, loose powder that remained on them and released in the air when being handled; this covered his wound dressing and open skin. A very serious, lifelong scar resulted. My father's decision and actions in the moment that one time resulted in terrible consequences that lasted for weeks and months.

When my father burned himself more than fifty years ago, today's medicine didn't exist. I was a teenager, and that episode caused big arguments between my mother and father for some time. She used to lament about how much more serious consequences could have resulted, and my father, in his defense and frustration, used to say, "I did not do that on purpose." From all these experiences, I continued to learn more lessons in life. Trying to help themselves out of their misery sometimes precluded a common-sense approach to a situation. Today, even after so many years of being an eyewitness to my parents' reality, I still can't believe they were able to face that part of our existence and move through it.

Thank you, Mom and Dad. I hope your souls rest in peace. Amen.

# Chapter 5
# Jovenado

When I left Italy, I was finishing the second grade, but because things don't always correspond in different countries and because I didn't speak Spanish when I arrived in Argentina, I had to return to kindergarten and begin again. I lost two years.

As you know, my father was determined to have me study and make something of myself. Like most young children, studying was not my priority. My father insisted on changing this because his profound belief was that through studying and education, you could achieve all that you want. It so happened that one day some missionary priests came to preach at a church a few blocks from our home. I was walking around and started talking with one of the priests. He showed me a pamphlet about the school they ran: the recreation, games and play, swimming in the river, and a picture of a pony the students could ride. You can imagine, as a child of approximately ten years of age, I was very taken in by these pictures and told my parents I was willing to go to this school. My father saw this as an opportunity of having the priests convince me to study and become somebody in life. Because of my parents' financial limitations, my father made a small contribution to get me into this school.

The purpose of this kind of school was to guide younger children in some way to become priests and at least have a vocation. At age eleven, I left for the school and spent seven difficult years there where the discipline was rigid, and you had to follow orders. I hated the hours of studying, constant prayers, and the long eternal Masses for our salvation, and I didn't like the Spartan environment. The first few months in this school were unpleasant. We had to continuously study, pray and hear Mass after Mass to no cnd. The sermons sounded as if the devil himself was present. They were always negative, telling us we could not do this, we could not do that; in other words, everything was bad. One thing that annoyed me very much was the long Mass on Sundays. We had to listen to three Masses followed by a sermon during which we were reminded of how fortunate we were to attend this school. I never came to understand this vocation.

Out of my anger and hatred for the school, I rebelled and was punished by being slapped in the face and sometimes kicked. Us boys were divided into two sections: one older group and one younger group. I was in the younger group when I started at the school, and we received punishment for every minor infraction of the priests' archaic rules. Sometimes we had to kneel before everyone in line, or our ear was grabbed and shaken like a leaf.

We were only allowed to speak to one another during recreation time. The corridors were to be completely silent, and even whispering was a punishable offense. There was little food available to us, and we had no independence. Another form of punishment was denying our customary piece of fruit during mealtime. Because so little was given to us to begin with, our bodies really felt the extra hunger after being denied this piece of sweetness. We were even denied fruit if we walked on the grass or dirt on the outdoor concrete patio. We would follow this penance because even though we didn't commit a sin, we all wanted to have a clear conscience. Today all this deprivation would be viewed as a form of child abuse. The intimidation used brainwashed us, making us timid and insecure. I became so shy and withdrawn that when visiting my parents, if someone came by, I used to blush and recoil in despair.

In my early days at the Jovenado, I was like a colt running free in the middle of the field with no purpose. I was young, averse to studying, and loved to be free, only wanting to play. When I was a young child, I remember my father telling me that when he was a boy, an orchestra would come to his town, and the violins, clarinets, and other instruments played such beautiful music. I never had the ability to play anything, so I was thrilled to learn that once a year, at the Jovenado, students like me could apply to study an instrument of their choice. Unfortunately, I wasn't doing well in my classes at the time; therefore, my application to learn the violin was rejected. This crushed me. I began to apply myself to my studies, and the following year I began studying the violin.

Once a day, we had recreation outside on the patio for thirty minutes, followed by another thirty-minute period during which we could read, play our instrument, or study. I always chose to play my violin and learned quickly. I was fascinated by the technique and skill of playing such an instrument and, in a short time, became part of the orchestra at the Jovenado. However, I was young and had difficulties with the timing of the music and certain introductions of the musical pieces we were playing. I would quickly become frustrated but was determined to succeed, and from that time on, my love for this genre of music became my guide. Many years later, I mentioned wanting to be a classical violinist to my father, and my father, being a practical person, explained unless I became the best in the world, this wouldn't feed me.

During those days, I felt like I would go crazy, but as time passed, I became curious. Boredom turned into curiosity. Each day as I turned the pages and read, I began to learn, and in this way, I became fascinated with the material I was reading, and to this day, it has lasted all my life. The teachings and education at that time were rooted in Middle Age thinking,* in which, if the Superior told you to jump from the window, you did not question him. The Church, at the time, had the compulsion to control one's free thinking, best proven by the index of book choices one was forbidden to read because the text of the books disagreed with the teachings of the Church.

Other books we read had pages where certain words and sentences had been blacked out. This was because one of the priests in charge felt that certain ideas expressed in certain books were not pure enough for our thoughts, and they controlled everything, even our thinking or what we could learn. The priests removed the writing of controversial ideas, such as those related to male development and hormonal changes. This is the environment I grew up in during those years. Of course, this was not realistic and did not give me any experience of daily life or any exposure to it.

Once a year, I was allowed to go home for one month to visit my parents. My vacation usually started as soon as exams finished in the middle of December. During that time, my poor mother found such joy in my presence she could not do enough to pamper me and cook the meals she knew I would enjoy. I think my mother had a special love for me. In comparison, my father favored my brother. My brother was not one to study. He enjoyed hunting and fishing and loved the outdoors. My father felt the same; therefore, they shared these things in common. My brother and I have always had different personalities. And because of that, our lives diverged in different directions (more on this later). I had challenging moments and although I was very close to my mother, knowing how sensitive and emotional she was, I was unable to be frank and tell her what I felt inside my heart because I knew it would upset her. Instead, I just painted a rosy picture for her because, although this was not true, I knew this was the best medicine for her soul.

I would return to school with a million regrets, missing my parents and the freedom other children seemed to have in the outside world. The first few days were always the most traumatic. We would all return around the middle of January, which is summer in Argentina. Classes didn't resume until the beginning of March, so the first six weeks were spent with the priests camping outside on a large property housing a monastery owned by the congregation where novices trained to be priests. This was several hours away from our school. We got there by truck; us younger ones were separated and put in the back of one truck while the older boys sat in the back of the other truck. We were forbidden to speak to the upperclassmen. Only new students were given a senior class member as a tutor for the first few weeks of school, and their communication was allowed for that short time only.

Upon arriving at the open field, we were separated into groups of five or six and erected our tents. Our mattresses consisted of straw. This was a disaster when it rained because the straw absorbed all the water, and the floors of our tents were dirt. We would eat outside under the trees, and one priest cooked all the food. He made a fire by digging a half-moon tunnel in the earth where wood was placed on one side and the smoke ventilated on the other. A large cauldron was placed over the center of the hole, which became our kitchen. Rainy days were difficult because we were given a bread sandwich with very little in the middle.

On days when the sun wasn't too intense, we would walk some distance to a nearby canal. The floor and walls of the canal were jagged, as this canal was created by water drainage from above into this flatter, low-lying land, and the water was murky because of the dirt floor. We were separated into two groups, not based on swimming ability, and the priest in charge would observe from a distance. I could not swim at this time. It's incredible to me, looking back, to note the complete ignorance of putting kids into the water with little or no supervision and with no knowledge of each child's ability to protect himself against the dangers of the water.

One time, when I was about fourteen or fifteen, part of a fallen branch was floating in the water close to the land's edge, and two or three boys were sitting on it. At some point, it cracked, sending all the boys off the branch and into the water. The boys started screaming because one didn't resurface, and they couldn't see him in the murky water. He was eventually found, and when he was brought out of the water, they placed him on the grass. Sadly, he had drowned. There were hundreds or thousands of mosquitoes on this poor boy, and this picture remains in my mind to this day. I had never seen a dead body before. I remember sometime later, there was a funeral mass, and from a distance, I saw this boy's distraught parents. It was horrible.

We were just children and teenagers at this school without any hint of compassion, love, or understanding. Everything was black and white. We were afraid to walk in the dark corridors at night, and on more than one occasion, when we were young, we would all sleep close together for comfort or because someone wet their bed. As the years passed and I was maturing, I had no answers to my feelings about growing up and what would be. Through the priest's regulations, everything was controlled. One of the rules was that two individuals could never stay together at any time. In the eyes of the priests, this was called "a particular friendship." Because of my tender age, this did not have any meaning to me, but to those guardians of morality, it was not the same. In turn, this influenced my future, causing me trauma I had to overcome. I was very timid. I was shy when I had to speak in front of others and very uncomfortable expressing my personal opinions. The school had no forum for public discussion and opinions.

The German priests came from the order of the Redemptorists. These priests had the power to decide your future and control your way of thinking. They thought and believed they knew what was best for you. The mentality of that time considered them to be Divine Inspiration; therefore, no one questioned them. A time did come, though, when I started to ask certain questions. These questions caused alarm among the priests because of their rigid beliefs and life. So much so that one day I was called to present myself in front of the school's Superior. He spoke with confidence. At that time, because of my family's financial status, of which he was aware, he thought the only way for me to succeed in life was to blindly follow the teachings of this order. He told me I would have a bleak future because I was not an intelligent person. Of course, I ignored his words because, at that age, I did not understand what he meant, but those words have been embedded in my mind forever. Thank God my future turned out differently than his projection.

In this place, as opposed to what nature shows you, you were on your own and your only guide. The innocence of youth was robbed by having to imitate the lives of saints who had lived well before our time and in a time of different cultures. At some point, we all became aware of our bodies changing or changes in a soprano's voice that was now becoming deeper. Although we couldn't explain why, we noticed our faces sometimes having ugly pimples, and, deprived of any explanation, I was often embarrassed by the thoughts in my mind concerning the opposite sex. I now know this is all normal and from the hormonal changes that occur in one's body during adolescence, but at the time, not being allowed to ask questions or given any explanation, you would lie awake thinking your thoughts during the evening were sinful. You felt the devil was all around you and the only way to clean your dirty soul was to go to Confession.

Because of these hormones and thoughts, I often had difficulty falling asleep because I finally had a moment to let my teenage mind and fantasies roam free. Being in bed at night seemed like the perfect place and time for the desire of the opposite sex to be more appealing. However, during the very early hours of the morning by what seemed to be an infuriated demon, but who was really one of the priests, I was awakened by the pounding on the floor of a military march and the clapping of his hands. I was left to go to Confession to calm my hyperactive mind. The next night would come again, and I would try to resist the temptation the devil was laying for me, but how long can an innocent, sweet, fragile mind resist such temptations?

Looking back on those days of confusion, growing up without guidance, we were left on our own to make our own decisions like a person lost in the middle of an ocean without having any reference or direction in which way to swim. Those were very sad days, but perhaps due to ignorance, following the blind teaching of someone that at one point had gone the wrong way, the tradition persisted, and when one recognized that those teachings might be flawed and tried to speak out, they were usually brought in front of a Superior, to be judged and repent; otherwise, this person was labeled a heretic, and the flames were ready to render justice to this corrupt soul.

You can't give what you don't have. As a grown man, I am convinced these insecure souls, the priests, did not have it because they never questioned anything; perhaps due to their ignorance, fear, or rigid upbringing, questions were not tolerated. I imagine the world our ancestors faced on a daily basis. What is even sadder is many times, in order for changes to occur, someone is usually required to use force. Lives are lost, families are destroyed, etc. The logical question is, why? Because the one who has the power in his hands is reluctant to give it up even though they know they are wrong. In my opinion, the medicine that can cure this 'cancer' is knowledge and better communication. This always opens peoples' minds, igniting the light to illuminate the darkness and allow clarity so we can all read the book of life.

Those years spent in the Jovenado left a deep mark on my character and forged a personality that took a long time to overcome the fear of the eternal perdition of being a sinner. I felt compelled to walk with my face looking down, as it was an insult to the Creator because he had created the sky with all its beauty. The birds, the flowers, and the fact that to deprive one of such joy in which nature could not be appreciated or admired, caused inner turmoil within me. Our tender minds at this early age were twisted so that we saw the devil in everything. I could only look up for hope but had none then, as everything was so dark Once a week, on Saturday, when we were allowed to shower, we had to line up and carry a bathing suit with us. We were told that when we showered in the stall, we had to wear a bathing suit in order not to sin. As time passed, I no longer paid attention to those archaic and silly rules. I began to shower like a normal person but made sure I left the stall wearing a wet bathing suit. I was happy to know I had good hygiene and didn't consider myself a sinner.

Looking back after so many years, I even remember eating in silence during our dinner hour at the school. During this silence, someone would read the life of a saint aloud and occasionally call our attention, by ringing a bell, to the fact that a student had been expelled. Unfortunately, because of the rigid nature of the school, no further discussion would be tolerated after this announcement. Although the intention behind the teachings was good, the priests were not qualified instructors, and the education was mediocre. Till the end of my days, I will question how the priest in charge of us children could be so cold and the person to save our souls. In the Spartan culture, to be king, children were trained to understand the human factor and to care for one another because this is the basic principle of survival. Instead, we experienced the opposite, which to me is ignorant, and renders the opposite of compassion and understanding, the guiding factors of humanity.

I remember one day when I was saturated with the education the school provided, with their archaic ideas and the impossibility of being able to develop into my own person, I returned home. When the school learned I was not going to return, they sent a priest to talk to my parents to try to convince them I should go back. My father could see how this school had turned me into a very timid individual. I was weak, had no self-confidence, and was not being prepared for the world. My father put his foot down and informed the priest that under no circumstances was I to return. It took me a long time to get rid of all those obscure ideas and the complexes that had tortured me for so many years.

I left the Jovenado and applied to the state school, E. Echeveria in order to finish my secondary education. The seven years spent at the Jovenado left me without any friends in the outside world and no one to offer me any possible guidance as to what to do. I went through a challenging time during this period of my life. As you know, the Jovenado made me very timid and insecure, and my self-confidence was non-existent. This was a huge impairment for me, in addition to preparing all summer for the exams I had to take in the fall. I was not looking forward to these exams, and my life was grim and uncertain.

I remember my parents spending most of their time in the center of the yard to try to provide me with a proper, quiet environment in which to study. From a distance, as I wove in and out of focus on my studies, I could sometimes hear them talking about me. When break time came, I would go outside to say hello to my parents; sometimes, they were unaware of my proximity to them. They were always happy to see me and clearly anxious about my upcoming tests in the fall. My mother, trying to hide the distress on her face, used to ask me in her sweet and simple way, "*Salvatore ai studiato?*" (Did you study?). I would, of course, say yes, to which she would follow up by asking, "*Ma tu ritieni lo studiato?*" (Are you able to remember what you have studied?) I would always aim to please her and assure her I did. She would bring her palms together and look at the sky in her own conversation with God. This always touched me because she was asking in her modest way for the *Signore faci questa grazia* (God, please give us help).

After some time, I retreated back to my studies, and for a few moments, more than once, I was able to meditate on what had transpired and how lucky I was to have such parents. They were simple in nature but reached deep into one's core to share their emotions. Like a car with a low battery that needs a jump start, this was the incentive for me, and with this new or renewed strength, I kept studying until my eyes were tired and my mind was saturated. I studied until my body was made aware that proceeding further was like pouring a cup of coffee into a mug already filled to the brim.

Looking back at my solitude in those days and my lack of friendships, I realize my desire to please my parents was a double-edged knife. Knowing full well what my parents were going through themselves and their incapacity to offer a better solution to help alleviate my dark moments, combined with my inability to be frank with them, knowing that would hurt them very much, I was left to portray a smiling face and hide my crying heart. With time I came to realize this was the price I had to pay for me to not adhere to the status quo. I knew if I could ascend out of that deep hole, I would appreciate and see who was making the light and turn my face to the sun.

With the beauty of hindsight and having lived many years away from the circumstances of the Jovenado, I now know some of the priests themselves had serious problems and were likely very afraid of losing the blind and irrational control they had based on fantasy and the unexplainable. I now realize their irrational behavior was a sign of their own frustrations, and perhaps they had doubts about the eternal decision to leave this world and questions about being told what to believe. I don't know if the Jovenado or similar schools still exist, but I certainly hope not because all youth deserve better than this.

*Galileo Galilei was an Italian mathematician who constructed his own primitive telescope and could see the mountains and valleys of the moon as well as Saturn's rings. This was a huge accomplishment at the time. He followed the Copernicus theory of heliocentricity (the sun is the center, and the earth moves around the sun). This contradicts the geocentric theory as described in the Bible. Galileo was brought to Rome as a sick, older man and had to present himself in front of the Inquisition, whereby he had to renounce his beliefs; otherwise, he would have been deemed a heretic. Galileo's famous saying, "*E pur si muove*," means the earth still moves around the sun. He stated this in front of the Inquisition, even though he was forced to tell them they were correct and renounce his beliefs.

Giordano Bruno was an Italian friar from the Dominican congregation as well as a philosopher, mathematician, and poet. He followed the Copernicus theory like Galileo. He thought the stars were distant planets that could possibly foster life, and the galaxy was infinite. He also was brought in front of the Inquisition, tortured, found guilty, and burned at the stake in Rome in 1600 because his beliefs didn't match those of the Church.

Girolamo Savonarola was another Dominican priest from Florence who spoke about the corruption of and defied the teachings of the Church. He was burned at the stake in Florence on May 23, 1498.

These three gentlemen and so many others were tortured or killed for defending their beliefs, and like Leonardo Da Vinci, they were ahead of the times during which they lived.

These men wanted to bring science and rationale to a time of ignorance and fanaticism. I think the judges of the Inquisition, who were a group of priests, delayed the Industrial Revolution by two hundred and fifty to three hundred years. To me, if they had open minds and allowed the people who had great knowledge to express themselves freely, a different world with improvements in the human condition, advances in combating diseases and education would have been made prior to the nineteenth and twentieth centuries.

Still today, five hundred years later, residual corruption and cover-ups exist within the Church. *Yerba mala no muere* (Bad grass never dies).

# Chapter 6
# Jovenado Part II

I went to bed this evening as always. For some unknown reason and without any logical explanation, I woke up, and for a long time, I could not fall asleep again. It seemed like something stored for a long time in my subconscious wanted to come out and scream its fury. I was not completely awake but in a state of limbo in which my mind was struggling, and although it wasn't clear, I was transported back to the days when I was very young, attending the Jovenado and reliving the struggles I had with math and the theorems of geometry.

My mind became conscious of a human figure, perhaps familiar, but kept at a distance due to my lack of understanding and missed information up to this point. This mysterious priestly figure eventually becomes clearer, and like a cold-case detective, I was able to solve the mystery after nearly sixty years have passed. I recall a German priest. Being so young, I don't think he was too advanced in age, but in some way, he looked it. Today, with a better understanding of that era, I would suggest he had aged prematurely and poorly, as his head was covered with whitish, ash-dry hair; his face with rim-eyed glasses reminded me of a Gestapo officer. This person walked in a particular way, with a stiff manner, as if his feet were brushing the pavers, and his back had some sort of hump, possibly due to arthritis, that in those cold days was formed by protecting himself against the weather with a big black coat wrapped around his body, which was reminiscent of Quasimodo jumping from one place to another, tolling the bells at Notre Dame cathedral.

I surmise from the characteristics of this person that he was also my teacher for math and geometry decades before, subjects of which I was never a friend, and perhaps because of my young age, my poor preparation, and lack of basic knowledge in these subjects, it was always a continuous sort of nightmare. During our classes, sometimes, this teacher used to go around and try to explain things further if one of us had a question. I remember I asked for explanations several times on topics I did not fully understand, primarily because of my poor background knowledge, but sadly the extra explanations may as well have been in a foreign language. I still didn't get it but would answer his questions in the affirmative. His lack of dental hygiene also didn't help. When he leaned over my desk to point to something and help me, there was an odor of decay that I can never forget. Again, as a young child, I was anxious to get out of this situation, which didn't help me focus. In reality, without the basic knowledge many of the other students had, any additional information was a waste. It was like painting a rusty iron chair that had been at the mercy of the outdoors and weather without first scraping the rust away. Today, although I am conscious of the reality of my poor educational foundations, because of my tender age then, to me, this person was a scary figure. I don't have to remind you that this was at a time and in a place where there were constant teachings of the devil being ever-present.

I have always liked history, and throughout my entire life, this appetite has increased tenfold. I love to learn and read about the past, and with the knowledge of today's world, quite often, I like to fantasize about the past and find pleasure in fixing and solving problems of those times and people. Using today's knowledge to solve ancient problems is a form of cheating. That being said, it makes me feel good, a poor consolation for a poor soul. At an early, innocent age, I was fascinated by the history of the Old Testament and the Romans and their conquests. In some way, I guess this is because we all like heroes, like Samson, who was able to kill hundreds of people just by using a donkey's jawbone. In another situation, during a fight of the Israelites against an enemy, because darkness was approaching, their leader was able to stop the sun from setting by holding up his arms, allowing them to finish the battle and defeat their enemy. In my innocent mind, there was a lot of admiration for these heroes who were superhuman in their power and intelligence and who were able to outsmart others. To me, these were very real stories. As I grew and began questioning the reality of these stories, the Superior admonished me. I was told I was not intelligent and would never achieve anything in my life. To think that in the Middle Ages, such types of questioning led to one being burned at the stake in the public square!

My early education was very poor, and my studies consisted of memorizing things. I wasn't taught to analyze or interpret things. I didn't have the luxury of having a teacher sit with me in a normal, civilized fashion and explain how things functioned. Sadly, this led to fear whenever my teachers posed a question to me. I was constantly worried and consumed by the thought of being struck on the head for giving the wrong response instead of taking the time to formulate a proper answer. This intimidation was not healthy. In Italy as an adult, I would hear, during various conversations, the notion of "*I figli si baciano cuando dormono.*" (the children are kissed when they are asleep.) The notion that affection can only be shown when a child is unaware would always make me think how distorted this world can be for an adult to hide the manifestation of their feelings of love for their own blood; what a tragedy. What distorted mind made this acceptable or even an accepted idea? I can only conclude that such unnatural ideas were fertilized because of the tremendous ignorance that existed throughout history. Referring back to the rusty iron chair not being scraped, this way of acting would make such a thick coat of paint one could not discern the original shape of the object.

These were my early educational experiences. Even after so many years, thinking about those days, having been alone and mentally isolated, I was like a small violet trying to grow, surrounded by tall grass. My tiny flower was prevented from seeing the sun's rays. I really don't know how I was able to make it in life. I think about history and how many minds and lives were ruined because of similar situations and circumstances. The waste of any human mind is horrendous when you think of the possible solutions a bright mind can introduce into this world, potentially alleviating misery and suffering that may plague some daily lives. All of this is something I have kept with me my entire life. My parents were never aware of the sad, dark days of my early age, and when growing up and talking to my mom, looking at her, I never summoned the courage to tell her my actual situation at that place. I always felt I would destroy the idealistic dreams she had made for me during all those years, and I thought this would be cruel and irresponsible.

Those teachers tried in their own way; however, they too were average in their knowledge and the methods employed were not normal or healthy. I think a supportive, warm word from those teachers would have done so much for our poor, disoriented souls. It has been over sixty years since my time spent at that school. I think even my own family will come to understand me better after knowing my actual experiences; for me to speak the truth after all these years has been cathartic. I am lucky to be the poor seed that was able to land in a desert and, by some miracle, flourish. As my granddaughter and all young people go through life, I wish and hope for her and them to look up and never despair because if I was able to find my way, despite the long, tortuous road, they will each have a much better chance to succeed in life, especially if they are fortunate enough to live in this wonderful land of opportunity, America.

# Chapter 7
# Bachillerato

After I left the Jovenado, I enrolled in a secondary school called Esteban Echeverria (National) to complete my studies and receive a degree called Bachillerato (this is the rough equivalent of graduating from high school in the United States). A diploma from this type of school was a requirement to enroll in a university. However, this was not without difficulty. The Ministry of Public Instruction did not recognize my private school education, and because it was the summer time, with sadness and desolation, I was forced to retake the exams of subjects equivalent to those of the previous two years, according to the curriculum of the public school. Because there was not enough time, I had to redo my third-year studies as well. I was behind and lost time once again. Of course, this affected me psychologically. It did not, however, deter my spirit and determination of looking toward and wanting a better future.

During my days at this school, I had many friends, some being the sons of the Estancieros, some were sons of lawyers and doctors — and I was the son of an immigrant. My early days at this school took me by surprise because coming from the Jovenado, where there was such rigid discipline, I found that here it was the opposite, and many times, the teachers were intimidated by those students who had influential parents. However, since the beginning of my time at this school, I noticed that some professors started to have good opinions of me because I was different; I respected them, and when called upon, I knew my subject. As a result, I did well at this school and received high grades.

Because my parents' house was on the outskirts of town, public services like transportation were limited. To get to National, I had to walk about three to four kilometers. On most days, I enjoyed getting the exercise; however, the first eight to ten blocks of this walk were not paved, and there were no sidewalks, so when it rained and the streets flooded, my shoes would immediately become soaked and heavy. Being young, I used to run from the front of one house to the next, resting when needed until I reached school. Unfortunately, the soggy feeling of my shoes would remain with me all day until I returned home, and my mother would dry my shoes with the residual heat of the oven once it had cooled from whatever she had cooked. One time I forgot to remove my shoes from the oven in a timely manner, causing the inner lining to crack. The next day I realized the new toughness of my shoes caused discomfort and my skin to blister. I should mention that I felt lucky at the time because I had proper shoes, and there were others who didn't and wore *las alpargatas* (a very basic, inexpensive sort of sneaker with a straw bottom and canvas covering).

During my two years at National, part of my curriculum required I attend physical education classes once or twice a week. This class took place around two or three in the afternoon in one area behind the public park in Azul, approximately four miles on the other side of town from where my parents lived. In order to get there on time, I would ride a bike. The bicycle I used was initially brought to Argentina when my Uncle Natalino and his wife came to Argentina, and we purchased it from them when they decided to return to Italy. This bicycle was a special possession for my family, and my brother and I had many arguments over who would use it each day as we shared this bicycle with each other and our father.

Despite my brother and I agreeing that he would always make the bike available for my use on my gym class days, there were many times when my brother didn't follow through, and I became increasingly frustrated. To make it to class on time, I would be forced to comb the local streets for my brother and our bike. Sometimes other older kids would think it was funny to all hop on our bike together and ride it around.

Between the jokes and too many wise guys clowning around, they would fight over the use of the bike, and they often wound up on the ground fighting. Despite some bruises and a lot of dust from the unpaved roads, luckily, no one suffered any broken bones.

Sometimes on the weekends in the late afternoon, I would meet up with six or seven friends from school in the town square. Usually, some girls from school used to join us, and we would hang out as teenagers do and at other times share in each other's birthday celebrations. Most of these young people were girlfriends and boyfriends, and I think I was considered somewhat strange or the outsider of the group because of my timidity and being a rather serious young man. As you know, a lot of this stemmed from my early education and how my formative years were spent. It took a long time for me to overcome the barrier of my shyness and for the more natural development of growing up to take over. Sometimes during these get-togethers, my contemporaries, trying to impress various girls, would mock others, and to me, this was very strange and cruel and always made me feel out of place.

I remember one day when I was around eighteen; maybe nineteen, the conversation was about the female menstrual cycle, something I had never heard about and was unaware of. Sadly, it was at this advanced age that I first heard of this. I hadn't been instructed about these things; in fact, I had been prevented from learning about the physiological natures of life. Upon returning home that day, I felt horrible; I was at my lowest of lows. I had no one to speak to about these things; I certainly would never dare to discuss such a topic with my parents. Although I didn't feel any malice, I felt inferior because I was not aware, worldly, or fancy, and it seemed no girl in her right mind would think of me or take me seriously. I couldn't help but feel I had a mark unknown to me that was visible to others, like the Roman slaves who, after escaping, when apprehended, were branded with a hot iron with the letter 'F' on their forehead for fugitive. I now know that solitude, poor self-esteem, and lack of self-confidence as a young man or woman can destroy a young person's mind. Although much is known and discussed these days about these important topics, in those days, the norm was to simply lower one's head and keep going without realizing this was perhaps creating an even bigger barrier and enlarging the emotional bruise.

One day, as I was approaching the end of this school, my parents received a small package for me from my Aunt Giuseppina. It contained a long-sleeve button-down shirt. This shirt was made of a material new to us. At the time, it was called lavilisto, wash and wear. I was in absolute heaven. I wore this button-down shirt each and every day. At night I would wash it by hand and hang it to dry. And sure enough, in no time at all, the shirt was dry, and I was able to wear it again. I wore this shirt for many years. Nothing like this existed in Argentina at the time, or at least anywhere we knew of or could afford. With time, the collar became worn to the extent that my mother, a very talented seamstress, removed, reversed, and reattached it. I wore it again so much that at one point, the long sleeves were made into short sleeves, and my skilled mother, who understood my love for this special shirt, created a brand new collar for me from the existing extra fabric from the original long sleeves. At some point, years later, when there was no longer any material to take and reuse, my mom was able to make a new collar with a section cut from the lower back of the shirt. That shirt survived for a very long time, but like most things in life, the day came when our separation was final. I did treasure it so, and it's the perfect analogy to my life at the time.

Aware of my parents' daily life, responsibilities, and my father's illness, I decided I would look for a summer job. This was no small matter because very few part-time jobs were available in Azul at the time. Through my uncle, Pasquale, I found out about a building company in need of manual workers. I applied, and I got the job. I soon realized that although I had helped my mother and father build our home, this was very different.

Approximately sixty kilometers from Azul, a millionaire bequeathed thousands of acres of land and livestock to the American Congregation of Carthusian Priests. These priests followed the doctrines of poverty and silence and had specifically come to

Argentina to build a monastery in the middle of this immense property. The area was different from the rest of the surrounding areas in that there were hills as opposed to flat land. When it rained a lot, the water from the hills created creeks and lakes in the valleys, making it very picturesque. To access this general area, there was a two-lane asphalt road. However, as one approached the entrance to this parcel of land, the road was no longer paved and only consisted of dirt. On the right side, the Carthusian Priests had built temporary shacks where they lived and prayed. There were approximately fifteen monks; most of them were young and came from poor families in the United States. Their lives started at 4 A.M. with meditation, prayers, and Mass. They had a meager breakfast and, by 8 A.M., took a truck ride to the top of the hill to start their daily work on the monastery alongside all of us.

The monastery was quite large. The style was of a European Middle Age look. It was made of bricks, and to my surprise, especially for that time, they had installed central air conditioning. I did not even know what central air conditioning was at the time. This is where I spent my summer from Monday to Saturday, working until late at night. I would leave on Monday morning around 5 A.M. My mother would prepare my lunch the night before. Then, I would have to walk several blocks to the main street and wait for a truck from the building company to pick me up. There were approximately twenty of us workers.

We sat in the back of the truck on stools. There was no roof, so we were exposed to all weather elements; however, when it rained, a canvas was put up and at least provided overhead coverage. When it rained and the canvas was on, some workers chose to smoke. I have always been highly sensitive to cigarette smoke, so that drive was very long and rather torturous for me. The trip took anywhere from two to two-and-a-half hours. The truck was old, and its speed was limited. Upon arrival, we started the day's work.

My job was to provide the brick and prepare the mortar. The bricks were not all the same. Some of them had defects, and before bringing them to the workers who had to apply the bricks to the façade of the building, I had to prepare and select each one for its perfection. I had to wet the bricks, and as construction progressed, I had to throw the bricks up to the workers. This was a new experience for me because my hands had not developed the callouses that the other workers had from their daily labors; therefore, the friction of the bricks against my fingers produced irritation, ulceration, and bleeding. This was painful. In the meantime, I noticed the monks used gloves to do manual work. When their gloves ended up with holes at the tips of the fingers, and they were not used anymore, they would throw them away. I would pick them up and try different ways to protect my fingers using the discarded gloves. I used to try the right glove on the left hand and vice versa or turn the gloves inside out. But all that was in vain because the gloves would not fit properly and ended up aggravating the situation even more.

As I described before, as one entered the property, the road became a dirt road. When it rained, and the dirt became mud, the loaded trucks carrying construction materials created crevices in the dirt. Once the weather cleared, and the earth was dry, the soil would become very hard. This made the ride more uncomfortable and unstable, so the trucks would bring rocks and dirt to fill in the crevices. The rocks were all different sizes, so my other job consisted of carrying rocks and dirt to fill in the crevices and smooth the road out as best as I could. What made this even more difficult was that some of the rocks were quite large and heavy, so needless to say, the labor was backbreaking. On more than one occasion, the driver would unload all the materials in one area. I suggested he leave the rocks and soil along different areas of the road to make the work easier. However, he chose not to do that, making the job more difficult for no reason, and the other workers would joke and laugh. Sadly, this was their entertainment. These men enjoyed teasing me because they knew I was planning to go to university to study medicine. For a manual laborer to even think about this at that time was a joke.

After the darkness settled, we would take the truck to go back home. Once I got home, I would take a quick shower, have dinner and go to bed. I was exhausted. Each morning I would repeat the same ritual. I did this for approximately ten days. It took a toll on me, so instead of coming back to my parents' house every night, I decided to sleep at the construction site in a tent. I took a sack filled with dried cornhusks to make a mattress. It was not the most comfortable place to sleep, between the quality of the mattress, heat, and mosquitos. For dinner, the cook on-site would make a big fire with wood, have a large cauldron going, and into this cauldron he would put sausages, corn, vegetables, potatoes, etc. Other times he would barbecue meat. We did not have a water supply; therefore, we could not shower. The water was brought in large metal containers twice a day, and we had to go with a cup to get water. Needless to say, this was not the most hygienic procedure, especially because the water was already warm given the hot summer temperatures.

It was during this summer that I needed a suit for university. However, with my work hours, I couldn't go to a store and try on a suit, so my father went to a store for me. The owner gave him three suits for me to try on one Sunday when I was home, and my father returned the other two the following week. I remember those days, being young and shy. People would come to visit and see the monastery being built. Some of these people were from Azul, and some were the parents of my contemporaries. I was embarrassed to be seen doing this manual labor and would hide so they would not see me. Years later, with all my life experience, I realize I should have been proud of myself for undertaking this job to help my parents. There was no need for embarrassment. But at that time, psychology was different, and people would judge you for doing this kind of work, not really understanding why.

I was paid every week and gave my salary to my father to help out. What I did not know was that my father took this money and placed it in a special place for me, as we did not have a safe or a bank account at that time. Looking back at those days in which I had only my aspirations and dreams, I believe all the inconveniences and harsh times made my character stronger and sharpened my will. I was more determined than ever to fight for a better future.

Years ago, when I would phone my brother in Argentina, he told me a friend of his, Miguel, was asking for me. Miguel was one of the men I worked with during the construction of the monastery, but I hadn't heard from or spoken to him since the early 1960s. So, one day, I decided to call Miguel, who was now of advanced age. Although he didn't realize who was calling in the beginning, once he realized it was me, he was overwhelmed with emotion and didn't even know how to address me (as, in his eyes, I was now a successful American doctor). I told him I was just his old friend, and we put aside the formalities and had a pleasant conversation. We reminisced about those early days, and he told me he was still in contact with some of the monks who live in the monastery. Sometimes, he said, when the monks came to town to buy supplies, they would stop by to say hello. He mentioned that one monk still remembered me and would inquire about me even after all these years had passed.

After some time, I decided to try to reach this elderly monk and phoned him in Argentina. I could hear his age and sense his frailness over the phone. For the first time, we spoke in English, and he said how happy he was to receive my call. He told me some of his family had moved and now lived in the Midwest, and if he were ever able to visit them, he would come to see me as well. Time passed, and one day, feeling nostalgic for my youth, I again phoned the monastery but sadly was told he had passed on. Rest in peace, Father.

# Chapter 8
# Universidad De La Plata

As the last weeks of school approached, one day, my father asked me what my plans were for the near future. I hadn't given much thought to this because my life had been operating in a day-to-day fashion. My father's question took me by surprise because I knew of my parents' financial limitations. I mumbled some words to the effect that, given the opportunity to continue my studies, I should become somebody and said some of my contemporaries were planning to go to the university to study medicine, and I would like to try too. I knew this was unlikely because I was the son of an immigrant, and my contemporaries' parents were doctors, lawyers, estancieros, etc., so this kind of adventure would be a major undertaking for my family and me.

At that time, I didn't have a clue about how to become a doctor and what was involved. To my bewilderment, my father liked the idea, and he and my mother were very supportive. I should say this wasn't without some resignation, for as you know, in the backyard of my parents' house in Azul was a large garden with different vegetables, a chicken coup with chickens who produced fresh eggs every day, and my parents also raised rabbits for consumption. In some very small capacity, you could say we were self-sustaining and had a tiny independent farm to help us through daily life. One day, my father was preparing a rabbit for my mother to cook. He was calling me, but I didn't want to join him because I didn't like watching him kill the rabbit and remove its skin. I overheard him commenting to my mother about how was I going to be able to deal with blood and other diseases when I couldn't watch him kill the rabbit we needed for food?

Nonetheless, my parents expressed their desire to help, and my mother looked at the sky and said, *"Sia fatta la volontà del Signore"* (God's wishes be done). They told me they would do anything to help, and I knew they were serious about it. That moment was, for me, the confirmation of what I knew was their eternal support, and for that, I never let them down. I made a silent pledge to them to do all I could, and I am proud to say I was always faithful to it.

Along with three other people I knew, I enrolled in the Faculty of Medicine in La Plata after obtaining my Bachillerato. La Plata is a cultural city built around 1882, with a population of more than seven hundred thousand. It has a big museum of paleontology, a large gothic cathedral, two famous soccer teams, beautiful stores, gardens with fountains, etc. When I got to the university, I lived in an old house owned by an elderly couple. The house had different rooms with a large patio in the front, covered with vines that gave us shade and helped protect us from the hot temperatures of the summer. More than fifteen students lived in this house (two to a room), and others often came by from different areas of interest to study. Sometimes, when the elderly couple was not around, some girls would also come by.

I was not accustomed to so much confusion and the coming and going of so many people. I was not able to concentrate. I remember a few older students who had been there for years. Although they could never seem to graduate or pass an exam, they took pleasure in continually questioning us about anatomy, etc., and intimidating us about our general studies. We were very young without experience and were easy prey for their tricks and laughter. One of these older students would pick one of us as a target and ask us questions about minuscule facts about our anatomy studies, and when we didn't have the correct answer, they would mock us, ridiculing the statement we made and telling us there was no way we would ever pass. We were naive, and of course, this made us nervous.

Up until this point, I had done well in school and received good grades; however, that sadly changed upon entering this program. Although I was a very responsible young man, I was timid and deeply afraid I would not be able to achieve my goal. Because of my upbringing and past experiences, I studied all day for long hours, and sometimes, without realizing it, I was not very productive and often read one thing all day without ever making sense of it. Looking back at this period of my life, I now see the idea of responsibility and doing the right thing had been so imprinted upon me that any deviation from it, or failure, made me feel guilty for wasting the meager amount of money my parents were able to give me as an allowance for meals, etc.

The sense of responsibility I felt towards my parents, who made tremendous sacrifices for me to attend university, left me preoccupied with not compensating them by my own success. I did not have a life. Only occasionally, because I have always liked soccer, I would go to watch a game not too far away from where we lived. While my contemporaries would go to Buenos Aires on the weekends to party and have a good time, I would lock myself in my room and study more. They would return Monday mornings around 2-3 A.M. and sleep the entire day. I never had the luxury of having my own set of books to study from; they were simply too expensive, so I used the class books available at the public library. I was able to check them out for a few days at a time. I recall the books being stained, and because the paper of these books was like papyrus, often pages were torn or missing altogether. On many of the pages, other students had written notes, and often it was very difficult to decipher the words. Nevertheless, I took notes to the best of my ability. In this regard, I took advantage of the opportunity my housemates offered me to use their books while they were away. It was so nice to have a personal set of books!

Approximately two miles from where we used to live, there was El Comedor Universitario. This was a nice building where we had our meals. More than five thousand meals a day were served, and it was very affordable. The lines started outside, and sometimes they extended for several blocks. While waiting, one was exposed to the elements: rain, heat, cold, etc. That was how we ate.

During my second year at the university, some girls from school who we were friendly with, on more than one occasion, invited my friends and me to a party at one of the girl's parents' homes. We would dance and have something light to drink. One day, at one of these parties, I met a young girl who was eighteen (I was twenty-one). Her father was a professor at the university's school of engineering. We dated for several months. Although I enjoyed her company, and it was nice having someone to talk to, I found my focus on my studies slipping. Because of all the distractions, we broke up and got back together quite a few times.

My friends also met girls during some of these events, and I often tutored them because they were slacking in their studies. On one exam that year, I did not perform well; that was the straw that broke the camel's back. I was so devastated by my performance on this exam that I ended the relationship and returned home to my parents. Today I can tell you I was depressed at that point. Between the stresses from school, not having proper books to study with, the distractions of dating, and feeling inferior from seeing how my colleagues lived all greatly affected me. At that time, however, such things were not as recognized, and therapists, medicine, and treatment were not readily available, especially to someone like me. My parents were very concerned and tried their best to help me, but I thought about quitting my studies, even though many of my friends came during this time to visit and encourage me to return to university. I spent my time at home helping my father with his garden and doing odd jobs for him, such as painting the house.

The experience of my first love affair left me, like it does almost everyone, with some scars. I was reluctant to go out for a while but, in time, met a few other girls; however, I didn't find myself having much in common with any of them. I have always liked the classics, like opera, but to others, it seemed as if I was from a different world.

During that time, on more than one occasion, I went out by myself. I thought a few times of returning to my first love, but it seemed destiny had other plans for me.

As the days passed, little by little, the clouds blinding me parted. I gradually found myself gaining energy and wishing to be back at the university. I began preparing once again to take the exam I had done so miserably on the year before. I did well and passed. This brought both my parents and me peace of mind.

This environment did little for my ability to concentrate or rest, and I found myself in a very unhappy situation. Our bedroom doors converged onto a shared patio where all the action was. There were usually some students kicking a soccer ball against the wall while others sat in a circle, drinking mate. Mate is a local drink similar to tea in which dry leaves, called Yerba, are placed inside a small container, and hot water is added. There is a straw or cannula with a filter at the bottom to drink from. Drinking mate is a social experience as the mate is passed around and around. Other students would play cards. All of this was like a circus to my mind and concentration, and one day I said enough of this nonsense. My friends and I decided it was best to leave this large, noisy house and rent another quieter place where we could focus and study.

We found another place that also had several rooms, but this time there was some control and order. After a while, because the owner liked us and saw we were responsible, we were put in charge of collecting the rent and keeping an eye on all activities at the residence. The downside was that the house did not have central heat and was very cold. I would often wake up in the middle of the night, not unlike my housemates, and put pants and other clothing on top of my pajamas. While we studied at our desks, we covered ourselves with blankets. No matter what, we were always cold. One day, while walking back from the university, we found an old kerosene heater someone had left outside, discarded with the garbage. As they say, one man's trash is another man's treasure, so we took the old kerosene heater, bought several feet of plastic tubing, connected the tubing to the kitchen gas, and brought the heat inside our rooms.

Although it was not the safest way to do things, we were young, cold, and had no other options. Looking back, it's a miracle no fire or other problems occurred.

A few times a year, I was able to visit my parents. Taking the bus was never an option for me — it was too expensive for my budget. However, I knew some truck drivers who didn't live too far from my parents' house, and I used to hitch a ride with them back and forth from the university. The distance was about three hundred kilometers, which took a while because the trucks were old and didn't move too quickly. It's not like traveling today! The trucks traveled in groups, and during lunchtime, the drivers would stop at restaurants along the highway to eat. They were reimbursed for their meals from the companies they worked for. I was often invited inside, but because of my economic circumstances, I would politely decline, saying I wasn't hungry, and wait outside, sitting under the shade of a tree. This was how I traveled back and forth from the university to my parents' house for seven years.

While I was a student at the university, I started to see how different people are. This was something I hadn't experienced before. I noticed there were students who studied hard and applied themselves, and then there were some who were just there to have a good time. Some of these 'good-time' students never even took an exam; their parents had no clue about this and sometimes didn't care. Most often, the students were there because they had wealthy parents who wanted their children to become professionals. At that time, it was a sign of prestige and went a long way for those with connections. This holds true in many places, even in today's world.

Sadly, I remember one very proud father who lived in a small town not far from us and his happiness in knowing his son would soon be graduating as a doctor. This father prepared a celebration and even arranged for an office to be opened where his son could practice medicine. It became apparent that there was a delay in his son's graduation, so one day the father decided to visit the university and inquire about the delay. He found out his son had barely attended classes and would not be graduating. This poor father took the train back home, and when the train stopped at one of the stations, the father exited and headed to the men's room. In his sadness and shame, because of the deceitfulness of his son, he hanged himself.

My parents could never visit me during my seven years at the university. They also never inquired about my attendance. They always had complete trust in me, and, being responsible, I never let them down because I knew how many sacrifices they made for me even to have the opportunity to study. In medical school, I quickly learned about specimens in anatomy classes, and in the beginning, between my running nose and teary eyes, it was apparent I was allergic to the formaldehyde used to preserve such specimens. In time, I got used to it enough and took medication to get through the class. During my many years of practice, my father never saw me in the operating room. He didn't see I had overcome that preliminary fear and could now handle so much more. What seemed unrealistic to him at one time had become my reality.

# Chapter 9
# Return to the Motherland

I graduated on December 18, 1968, after spending seven years at the Universidad de La Plata with a Doctorate of Medicine degree. Facing a decision on what to do next and the uncertainty of a stable future, I decided to return to my birthplace, Italy. I did not feel there was a future in Argentina for me, whereas in Italy, I was hoping to specialize. My life in Argentina resembled a crab, moving one step forward and one step backward. The life of complacency that existed there at the time was not for me. Instead, I found polluted ideas flourished. I wanted something solid for my future life. And so, reluctantly, I left my family and went towards my questionable future.

In preparation to have my degree recognized by the Italian state, I had to have my diploma certified and recertified by many different authorities in Argentina and take four exams in Italy. After obtaining the diploma certifications, they had to be translated into Italian and sent to Italy. The Italian Embassy would then be in charge of sending all the documents to the University of Naples, where I chose to take the four exams.

For two months after being informed of these requirements, I did nothing else but go back and forth from La Plata to Buenos Aires, each day, in the heat of the summer, going from one ministry to another to have a seal printed on the back of my diploma and pay the necessary fee so it could be sent to the next department in Buenos Aires. This took a lot of patience and standing in line for days. The windows and departments where such seals and stamps and fees were paid closed for lunch each day. Sometimes, the person I needed to see was on vacation or simply not in the office. Back and forth I went, with all of this creating a lot of anxiety.

Finally, after many weeks, I was able to gather the documents that needed to be translated. I was scheduled to sail to Italy the following week, but because my documents had to be translated beforehand, I had to beg a translator for this special favor. My appointment was late in the afternoon, and I vividly recall it being a hot summer day, and I was so exhausted I lay down on the grass in one of the park squares and cried like a small child.

I arrived in Italy at the beginning of March. Upon arrival, it gave me great joy to see relatives and cousins I had not seen for years or decades. They helped me in the best way they could and were very accommodating. However, when I got to the University of Naples, I was informed I would have to wait until September to take the four exams because the scholastic year was ending very soon. My frustration and uncertainty returned, and I faced yet another hurdle to overcome.

As you now know, Scauri is a summer resort with a beautiful beach and many tourists. Each day I would walk to the beach to clear my head and talk to different people. One day I ran into a distant cousin of mine who was living in the United States. He was familiar with my situation and encouraged me to come to the United States. I thought about it. I wrote to my other cousin, who was also presently living in the United States, and she told me to come too. My extended family, in fact, all agreed I should go. My Uncle John and Aunt Petrina, along with their two teenage sons, were kind enough to offer me a place to live with them in their home in the Bronx, New York.

I was convinced and once again packed up my bags. I touched down at Kennedy Airport in Queens, NY, one gray day in November of 1969. The only impressions or images of the United States I had ever seen were those on television and in Hollywood movies. I remember being amazed at the piles of garbage while traveling from the airport to my cousin's home, although I later learned a sanitation strike was going on at the time.

When I arrived in this country, it was a memorable day for me; filled with new hopes, dreams, and aspirations. As the days passed in this new land, my experiences gradually convinced me I had finally arrived at the place of my long-awaited future. As it turned out, this land would be the crowning point of my life. Quickly I discovered what this country could give and allow me to do. I was finally smiling because, in comparison to my previous experiences, this was a positive one, and I decided I would work very hard to reach my goals. This was not without heartache; there were many bridges to cross and so many streets to walk.

After my first week in America, my cousin's husband came to pick me up at my Uncle John's house in the Bronx and take me to Stamford, Connecticut, to visit the rest of the family. It was here I witnessed something previously unimaginable to me. My cousin, Antoniette, took me for a ride in her car to show me around, and, to my disbelief, we wound up at the local public library. I was flabbergasted upon entering the library. Antoniette took me to the music section, and for the first time in my life, I saw a whole record section of various operas. I can't even describe the sheer volume of emotions this created within me. Antoniette then told me I could take a few to borrow for a time to enjoy listening to them at home. I was beside myself with glee!

I spent most of that week inside, reading the librettos of the operas and listening, over and over, to Mozart, Verdi, and some works of Bellini. I was as close to being in heaven as a living human being can be. During those days, I was like a child with a new toy, but unlike a child who tires and places the new toy aside, I, on the contrary, became more and more attached to the operas the more I listened to them. Like a wearisome traveler finding water in the desert, the knowledge of such treasures being so close to me in this county confirmed I landed in the right place and stimulated my desire to succeed here.

I didn't speak English, and although I had studied the basics in school, I never thought to pursue it because I did not have the slightest idea that one day it would be indispensable. The first thing I had to do was to learn and master the language. So, with money borrowed from my family, I took courses at New York University (NYU) for several months. I also spoke English with my cousins, aunt, and uncle as much as possible and started watching American TV. The medical diploma and degree I had were not automatically recognized in the U.S., so I was required to pass the ECFMG (an exam given in the United States and worldwide to foreign doctors and American graduates outside of the US). After passing this exam, I would be allowed to apply to hospitals to start specialization training in surgery that would last five years. Unfortunately, during my training, I had never heard of nor experienced exams with multiple-choice answers. To me, this type of questioning was very confusing and frustrating. My anxiety came back, and the psychological wound began to bleed again.

This was a challenging moment in my life because, again, it seemed the door was closing in front of me, and I did not know what to do. However, in view of my limited possibilities and my previous history, I had no other choice but to face this situation and try one more time to climb that mountain that had been so difficult for me in my life. Again, in order to understand how to take these exams, I had to take refresher courses at NYU, and again my family had to come to my financial assistance.

The immigration law at that time was very specific. I had to apply for a special permit to remain in the U.S. and continue my specialization. I had to hire an immigration attorney, and at the time, I was spending a fortune on this attorney. Again, I needed financial backing. Logically, in time and when my situation finally improved, I paid back all my debts. I really do not know how to thank all my family, and they will forever be in my heart.

Finally, the day of my exam arrived. Needless to say, I was very anxious. I went to take the exam in a hotel in downtown Manhattan with more than a thousand other doctors. These exams were a nightmare for me. Even after so many years, this exam and the many subsequent exams I had to take continue to give me nightmares every now and then. They seem to be so real, and although they last for only a few seconds, to me, it seems an eternity, and I wake up shaken. Only when I am fully awake and aware of what is going on can I take a full breath and know all is OK.

The first time I took the exam, I was not aware that the exam was timed, and I did not fully understand some of the questions because of my limited understanding of the English language. I was tired and exhausted and used to go more than once to take a break and drink water. At one moment, the proctor announced, "You have half an hour to complete the exam." Well, put yourself in my situation. My anxiety and desperation settled in, and I still had more than half of the exam to complete. I had no choice but to mark random answers to the remaining blank questions. Of course, I felt very down. I was frustrated and morally defeated. I was down and did not have anything else to do but wait several months for the results.

Not surprisingly, I did not pass. My family, seeing me suffer, tried to encourage me in their own way. I felt like an inconvenience to my uncle and his family because I lived in their home, so I would walk for hours outside in the freezing cold. I didn't care. I was miserable and had no peace of mind. I often thought of how I would have to lie to my parents and say everything was fine when, in reality, everything was not even remotely OK. With my uncle and cousins' encouragement, I started to study night and day in preparation for the next exam after a few days. The only breaks I took were my continuous walks in the cold. It seemed the cold air and wind hitting my face and ears, eyes wet with tears, was some sort of catharsis. Only God knows how heavy my burden was.

I believe in one's own destiny, but at this juncture, my trial was too much to confront. I recall one day speaking to one of my cousins and telling her I would attempt to pass the exam one more time, and after that, I would have to return to Italy, but in doing so, I would be a defined person and do what I had to do there. I told her I would only leave if the doors in the United States were closed for my future! Then, I remembered some words from the opera *Lucia Lammermoor*, "*Dei giorni di amaro pianti*" (Those days of bitter tears). Not being able to see an end to my misery and with no hope of a bright light on the near horizon, my cousin was able to ease my pain and reignite my hopes.

My aunt and uncle's house was modest, and because my cousins were two teenage boys, the TV was always on when they were home, and it was difficult to find a quiet place to study. I found my quiet place in their boiler room, of all places, where I would sit at night, studying and translating whatever I still couldn't understand so that it made sense to me. Oddly enough, this boiler room was my refuge and the witness of my early days in America. I would sit there and remember, some time ago, when in Argentina in similar situations, I would tell my mother, "Mom, I believe one day the sun is going to shine for me too!"

I went to retake the exam. I was not certain how well I did, but compared to my previous experience, it was a positive one. Today, I realize I never truly learned how to study correctly until coming to the United States, primarily because when in the Jovenado, the system was simply to memorize things. We were not taught to interpret or analyze the material in our minds. While I waited for the results, I had good and bad days. I waited every day, for about two to three months, for the mailman to arrive. When I heard the click of the mailbox, I would run downstairs and pick up the mail, but that particular letter seemed to take forever to arrive. I understood, at this time, what my mother went through in Argentina in her desire to have some news from Italy. This situation was like life or death to me because my entire future depended on passing this exam.

On some of the weekends during this time, I would travel to Stamford, Connecticut, to visit my cousins and Uncle (Zio) Luiggi and Aunt (Zia) Giuseppina*. Zia Giuseppina was my father's older sister. We would all cook and do some yard work together. My cousin, Antionette, the youngest daughter of Zio Luiggi and Zia

Giuseppina, used to bring extra work from her place of business, and I was happy to assist her in order to make a few dollars. Cousin Antionette's husband, Nicolas (Nicky), enjoyed hunting, and on more than one occasion, I went hunting with him in upstate NY. Here, I could see large tracts of land with many apple trees. I have always enjoyed the outdoors, and this new experience refreshed my mind. Nicky was hunting deer on one of our first visits upstate. He told me to go in one direction while he went in the opposite direction. I kept walking and walking until, at some point, I must have ventured well onto someone's private land. This man came up to me and was talking to me, but because of my limited English, I had no idea what he was saying. He kept looking at me as I was gesturing with my hands. Thank goodness my cousins were looking for me and came to save me.

In preparation for these trips, Antoniette used to prepare enormous sandwiches for all of us that we always ate very quickly because of the cold. We would wake up at 4 A.M. to take the long ride upstate and return with our shoes and socks wet and our bodies tired. We would hop in Nicky's station wagon, turn the engine on and get the heat going. These were enjoyable and memorable adventures.

Aunt Giuseppina was like a second mom to me as my own mother was across the ocean and far away. During those weekends in Stamford, Connecticut, she would often prepare my favorite meals for me and try to comfort me. Zia Giuseppina was a simple lady with a good heart. She was, until her last days at nearly one hundred years old, the engine behind her entire family. She was a model of inspiration and close to my heart because she had the intuition to see and read my feelings. I can't thank her enough for always believing in and encouraging me. She was always the center of the party whenever we were together. She used to sing old Italian songs, some of them being very nostalgic to me. We had good times. Sometimes, when the entire family was all together, many cousins and some other Italian friends, we used to have a picnic at the park and on the beach in Stanford. These days were very special for me because temporarily, I could forget my misery and the terrifying question I never seemed to be able to answer: what would be of my future?

I had heard if you passed the exam, the paper was green. So one day, the mail arrived with an envelope addressed to me from the licensing board, and I could see the green paper showing. No words could describe my joy as I read the congratulations on passing the exam. My family and I celebrated. This was only one exam that gave me the opportunity to begin my specialization. Thank God I was not aware of what was still to come. But, that is for another day.

My Aunt Giuseppina decided, on her own, as she had been the family's leader for years already (as her father was lost for some time during the war), that she was old enough to marry at fifteen years old. After the war, she noticed the lack of available jobs for her husband, Luiggi, who used to make carriages to transport raw materials to the ceramic factory to make bricks and tiles. Before the war, in Scauri, there were only a few trucks, but with the war ending and the beginning of reconstruction, everything started to change, and my uncle was out of a job. My aunt, always ahead of her time, heard of openings in migrating to America, applied for them, and moved as soon as they were granted entry to this country.

In moving to the United States, my aunt left two of her daughters in Scauri with their respective families as they were already married. She and Uncle Luiggi had four children: three girls and one boy. My aunt, lying awake at night and thinking of her children, decided to become a United States citizen so she could reunite the family and bring all of her children here. Although she had little schooling and had to study at night in her spare time, she achieved her goal and became a U.S. citizen well into adulthood.

Aunt Giuseppina got a job as soon as she arrived in this country and worked for many years until retirement. However, after a short time, she was bored and decided to find another job. She found a job as a housekeeper at a local hospital. She was diligent and caring, and everyone loved her. So much so that years later, when it came time for her to retire again, the hospital threw a party in her honor. She was asked to say a few words at this party, and when she got up, in front of her friends and, in her Italian accent and with a smile on her face, she said she had an apology to make. Everyone was shocked and wondered what she was going to say. She said humbly that she had lied about her age on her original application because she thought if anyone knew she was older, she would not have been hired.

Not wanting to inconvenience or depend on their children anymore, as my Uncle Luiggi didn't drive, Aunt Giuseppina decided to learn and obtained her first driver's license at sixty-eight so her husband and she could be independent and run their errands. Aunt Giuseppina was a formidable woman until she passed at nearly one hundred years old. We all miss her very much. May she rest in peace.

# Chapter 10
## Specialization

After receiving the fantastic news of passing the examination, I started looking for hospital residencies. I was accepted by Misericordia Hospital and Fordham Hospital, both in the Bronx. However, after being accepted by these hospitals, I had to wait until July to start my training. In the meantime, not having any income, I learned that Misericordia was looking for a lab technician (phlebotomist) to draw the blood of current hospital patients, so I applied and was accepted for the job. Although I don't recall my exact work schedule, I believe I was drawing blood at least two times a week for two hours each day. I would wake up at 4 A.M.; walk several blocks to the main road to wait for the bus, and later switch to a second bus that dropped me about one block from the hospital. I was paid five dollars for every two hours of work, and I was in heaven with this new job of mine. I remember I spent almost half my week's pay on transportation fees, but I didn't care. I was out of the house and had a job for the first time in this country. My American dream had just started.

I began my one-year internship and quickly understood what it was to be an intern. It was like a rigid military program. Most of my time was spent caring for patients and assisting in the operating room. I spent many hours standing on my feet and was taking calls every other night. This meant that I worked every other day and had to be available both that night and the following day. The hospitals where I interned were very, very busy. The nights I was on call, I was almost always up all night between caring for the people in the emergency room and patients on the surgical floor. During this time, many patients with severe conditions required intravenous fluid (IV), and there was a constant demand for me to start such IVs. On many occasions, IV fluid bottles ran empty before they were changed because the nursing staff was so busy and overwhelmed. When this happened, the catheter could clog, so I would have to restart the IV. This was not always easy because some patients had poor and compromised veins.

A demanding schedule and lack of sleep can affect anyone's temper or cause attitudes to shift; however, I quickly learned it was a must, at all times, for the nurses to be treated with the utmost respect and friendliness. There is a saying from Martin Fierro (gaucho poet) *"Hacete amigo del juez, y no les de que quejarse porque siempre es bueno tener palenque donde rascarse"* (Become friendly with the judge and do not let him have any complaints about you because he controls the situation).

Despite being exhausted after a night on call, when I finally returned home, I was unable to sleep because of being so overstimulated. So I would usually just rest my legs while I closed my eyes and think about how lucky I was that I had passed the exam and now was an intern. Unfortunately, more than one of my colleagues didn't have such luck, and some, already having families to support, had to work while they were studying; therefore could not put in the time I had to study. I felt sorry for them. Some of these colleagues worked in Misericordia and Fordham as technicians and called me doctor as I passed in the hallway. Knowing many of their stories, I knew several tried to pass that exam on more than one occasion. I understood their frustration very well and tried to give them hope and encouragement. Realistically though, time was not on their side.

During training and being an intern, you are at the bottom of the totem pole and have to deal with the pressure and frustration of the chiefs of various departments and the other, more senior interns. Sometimes, just as the day seemed to be coming to a close, the Chief Resident would page me. He would send me to get all the lab reports from the patients' charts because the Chief of Surgery was coming to make rounds with us in fifteen minutes. The Chief of Surgery would ask questions, and we would all make sure to respond in a way as favorable as possible to the Chief Resident; otherwise, the Chief Resident would let us know his annoyance in one way or another as the one on the top oversees those on the bottom and calls the shots. As the weeks passed, I began to learn how this system worked, and not being used to it, I adjusted to it, little by little.

My schedule and the work I did as an intern were exhausting, and unfortunately, it took many years for the authorities to recognize the working hours of an intern were not safe or acceptable. The protracted hours allowed at that time affected decisions regarding patients' lives and recoveries. Although not during my time as a resident, years after I finished my training, changes were made to the length of time an intern was allowed to work.

After this one-year internship, I applied to the residence program at Cooper Medical Center in Camden, New Jersey. This medical center is and was, even then, in a very poor area. Crime was rampant. We saw gunshot and stab wounds on a daily basis, and we spent many hours in the operating room saving lives. Although this was a sad commentary on human society and inner-city, poor neighborhoods, I acquired an amazing skill set as a surgeon. It was akin to operating on a battlefield, and I was very fortunate to have received such excellent training. My judgments and ability to make the correct decisions in extreme situations under pressure continued to be a huge asset for my future practice.

I will say it was also at this juncture, and it first started when I came to this country, that I achieved some security in my character, which was not easy. I began to see how life expresses itself and how it's OK to be selfish sometimes and be strong and ask questions. The ice had started to melt and was now a puddle.

# Chapter 11
# My Residence At Cooper

After completing my one-year residency, I needed to find and apply to accredited hospitals offering a surgical specialization program. I chose and was accepted at Cooper University Hospital, located in Camden, New Jersey (adjacent to the Delaware River). The program I chose was a five-year program. During the five years of intense training, I saw and treated cases in three areas of surgery: trauma, general and vascular, on a daily basis. After a few months, it became standard routine and procedure to take care of patients who were sick or wounded because of many different reasons.

During those five years, I was exposed to so many multiple emergency situations and also regular cases such as inflamed appendixes, explorations of the abdominal cavity and the removal of gallbladders containing stones, that if left untreated, can cause multiple issues such as fever, pain or blockage of the bile duct, etc. This was all work done by a general surgeon. As vascular surgeons, we did open heart surgery, removed clots, or corrected blockages when the arterial circulation had been compromised (removal of the clots is an embolectomy using a small catheter balloon or, if needed, bypassing the obstruction using the patient's own veins or Gortex tubing). A vascular surgeon also does work like removing varicose veins in the legs. A trauma surgeon deals with injuries caused by motor vehicle accidents, gunshot or stab wounds, or injuries caused by falling from a high place, etc. I studied and learned how to handle all three of these areas and their respective surgeries.

My day always began by making rounds before 7 A.M., sometimes a bit before that, but always based on the surgical schedule, and was followed by surgical cases in the operating room. Some days we also had to attend lectures or other such conferences. The surgery cases I worked on were either general in nature, as discussed above, or working with the cardiac team doing open-heart surgery. Many times during those long days of surgery, I was not able to eat lunch. By the end of the day, I would feel a migraine coming on. I learned to carry hard candy, so in between cases, I would have one or two until I could have dinner, and most of the time, by doing this, I could ward off the headaches.

As a resident, I was responsible, like all the other residents, for taking night calls every other day, which put us on call for a straight twenty-four hours. This translated into doing surgical cases by day and having my responsibilities continue through the night right into the next morning. I worked in the emergency room on the off nights when I was not on call because I needed to make money. Cooper Hospital's emergency room was always very busy; therefore, I was up most of those nights too. If I could squeeze in one hour of sleep on those nights, I was a lucky guy. Even though it was my choice to work in the emergency room, I still had to start the next morning doing my daily resident routine. There were many, many days in which I was up for more than twenty-four hours. At that time, though, I was young, full of energy, and determined to fulfill my dream of being a surgeon.

To practice medicine in the State of New Jersey, I was required to pass a three-day exam to obtain a federal license. The exam to obtain this license was called the FLEX exam. If I passed this exam, then and only then could I practice medicine. I studied vigorously for this exam whenever time allowed between cases and working. Those exams were really a nightmare for me because they tested all the subjects I had learned years ago in medical school in Argentina. Obviously, many years had passed since then, so there was a lot of refreshing to do. The FLEX required skill, knowledge, and timing. For me, at my age, it was an insurmountable barrier to break through. Just the preparation for those exams caused tremendous anxiety and stress. Despite being fluent in English at this point, the way certain questions were phrased remained very puzzling to me, and not having studied in this country again made this task more difficult.

During my residency, in December of 1974, I returned to Argentina because my brother was getting married. I finally saw my parents after not seeing them for years. This was years before the age of cell phones and virtual calls, so when you didn't see someone, you genuinely didn't see them. I was also anxious to see my friends from high school. I remember way back when many of them would come to dinner at my parents' home, and we would all enjoy a good, home-cooked Italian meal. That visit back to Argentina was a combination of happiness and disappointment. As it wound up, I didn't end up spending nearly as much time with my old friends as I had hoped. In fact, it seemed my decision to leave Argentina and pursue a life in the United States had created a divide between them and me. It was obviously wonderful to see and spend time with my parents, though.

Throughout my residency, I was required to work with different teams of doctors. After returning from Argentina, I was assigned to work with a well-known surgeon. One day, while I was in the operating room, I was told of a post-surgical patient who was now experiencing complications and unable to eat. This patient was in need of intravenous fluid administration. Apparently, after some members of the IV team and a handful of residents were unable to help him, I was told to go and see this patient. I remember, as if it were yesterday, walking into the room and seeing the patient sitting in a chair on the side of the hospital bed. He had different tubes coming from every which way, and he was pale, had big scared eyes, and his arm was swollen and black and blue. I introduced myself and noticed he had an Italian name. So I began to speak in Italian, and sure enough, we started to engage in a conversation.

He informed me he was a classical pianist and was now the Dean of the Philadelphia College of Performing Arts. As it turned out, he had been in Italy during the war as a Lieutenant Colonel in the U.S. Army, and after the war ended, he was put in charge of overseeing the rebuilding of the famous opera house, La Scala in Milan, Italy, as Allied forces had destroyed the opera house during the war. Because of my love for classical music, I felt a tremendous affinity toward him from the moment I met him. He went on to tell me he was friends with Toscanini, the gentleman who was the conductor for the inauguration of La Scala after the rebuilding was complete, and he had even gone to Switzerland to pick up Toscanini, who had traveled from New York, where he resided, to bring him to Italy in preparation for this event.

Our ongoing conversation and exchange apparently relaxed him, and when the tension subsided, he looked at me like a friend. Finally, it reached a moment when with his big eyes, he said, "Okay, doctor, you can start the IV now." The amazing thing was, after all the previous attempts, I was lucky enough to have been able to get a vein and start the IV without him even realizing it while we had been chatting. As a believer in destiny, it's not that I was such an expert at starting an IV; I just happened to get lucky that day. From that day on, that patient and I became very close, and he trusted me. He had renewed hope in life, and I would eventually come to meet his wife and their daughter, Roberta.

Every day, and several times during the day as needed, I used to go to visit him to make sure things were progressing well. During some of these visits, his wife would be there, and we would have many conversations in Italian and exchange many of our cultural thoughts. We spoke about history, shared ideas, life, etc. Late in the afternoon, when I used to visit my patients, on more than one occasion, I saw a beautiful young lady. She was eventually introduced to me as the daughter, Roberta, of Mr. Petrillo, the man and patient I had become friends with. Roberta was a special education teacher, and I was taken in by her beauty and manners and was very impressed. I started to think about her. In the meantime, the moment came when Mr. Petrillo's complications ceased, and we could remove all of the tubes; he was finally able to eat. Shortly after that, he was discharged and allowed to return home.

Shortly after being discharged, Mr. Petrillo and his wife were invited to a private concert. His circle of friends were mostly musicians, and because of this, Philipe Entremont, Najia Sonnenberg, and some other well-known musicians would be at this event. Mr. Petrillo phoned me, stating he was not quite up to going to this and that he had asked his daughter to go in his place and to bring me, the "resident who took such good care of him." I was beside myself with joy and excitement! That was the beginning of my relationship with Roberta. The event was held in a beautiful, private apartment, and to me, the whole thing was overwhelming: the luxury, design, and overall beauty of everything. I certainly had never been exposed to this before. All this, combined with my new, beautiful companion, gave me such peace and solitude. When the concert was over, we met up with Roberta's parents, who were at the Naval Base in Philadelphia. We joined them for dinner and danced the night away. I remember asking Roberta while dancing, "Did you ever think you would be dancing with the guy in the scrub suit?"

As my relationship with Roberta progressed, one weekend, while having dinner with my soon-to-be in-laws at a restaurant in Philadelphia, my beeper went off (this was the method of reaching doctors at the time), notifying me of a gunshot victim who was bleeding in the emergency room and needed emergency surgery. After giving my surgical attending all necessary instructions, Roberta quickly drove me to the hospital. As we pulled into the parking lot, my attending was also getting out of his car. He asked Roberta if she had ever been in the operating room and if she would like to accompany us. This was clearly something she hadn't expected, but after being introduced to the nurses in the operating room, she changed into the surgical scrubs provided and received a few elementary instructions about not touching anything as everything is sterile in the operating room.

It was the first time she witnessed me operating. Roberta could see what was going on, and I later remember she was excited to recount to her parents how we exposed the contents of the abdominal cavity. Like a person looking for a small object inside a box, the most efficient way is to remove all its contents and explore it step by step while ensuring a clear view. We removed all of the clots and controlled the bleeding caused by the bullet. After the bloody area was cleaned, we would have a better view of the abdominal cavity, the intestines were brought out, and a meticulous exploration was performed to ensure the bullet hadn't torn the bowel and any necessary repairs were made. When she described all of this to her parents, this having become the daily routine for me, it sounded so miraculous. Seeing how impressed she was by my performance of the surgery stimulated my ego to become an even better surgeon because in her eyes, although she didn't consider me a god, perhaps I could be viewed a few steps below that of a semi-god and that would be sublime to me.

# Chapter 12
# End of My Residency &
# the Beginning of My Career

During my last year of surgical residency, when I was the chief resident, I got married. After so many years of fighting and spinning in circles, it felt great to be approaching the peak of the mountain, so to speak. My in-laws planned a magnificent ceremony, and my parents came from Argentina to the United States for the first time; the things they saw and learned mesmerized them.

Roberta and I were married at the Naval Base in Philadelphia and had our reception in the Officer's Club. My family from New York and Connecticut came as well as family from my in-laws' side. We invited friends, Roberta's school colleagues as well as the Chiefs of Surgery, and my surgical residents and colleagues. My father-in-law, being a retired Lieutenant Colonel, wore his dress uniform from the Army. He looked fantastic.

After returning from our honeymoon in Florida, we lived with my in-laws in Cherry Hill, New Jersey, for one year, which allowed us to save some money to start our future once my residency officially ended. During the end of my five years at Cooper Hospital, another colleague and I shared the position of being the hospital's chief resident, and for that entire year, we alternated all the hospital calls. I would take calls from home, and if any problems occurred, the fourth-year resident would contact me. Then, if needed, I would return to the hospital, render my opinion, and if and when a patient needed surgery, all the necessary preparations began. My surgical attending was notified, and when given the okay, the nurses in the operating room and the anesthesiologist were notified, and we made sure the lab had blood ready in the event a blood transfusion was needed.

Some nights, being young and ambitious, Roberta and I used to travel to quite a few remote places so that I could do physical exams for different insurance companies. There was no GPS or navigation at the time, so my wife and I relied on maps. Sometimes where we wound up was so remote it was not indicated on the map, and we became lost and had to slowly find our way home. Looking back at those days, the time and fuel spent traveling, examining patients, and the dangerous places we ventured to, alone with my young, beautiful wife, to be paid twenty-five dollars for each report, I realize how lucky we were not to have been injured.

Oddly enough, during this time in my residency, a colleague from Argentina, who graduated from the plastic surgery program, moved to a town named Teaneck in the northern part of New Jersey. He invited Roberta and me to visit him and his wife one weekend. He showed us around. We came to like the area very much, so it became my intention to start my own surgical practice in this area once I completed my residency. Teaneck is located in Bergen County and very close to New York City.

During this last year of my residency, I applied to various hospitals in northern New Jersey. I applied to, among others, and was accepted at Holy Name Hospital in Teaneck, St. Joseph's Hospital and Barnett Hospital in Paterson, and Valley Hospital in Ridgewood. Later, I came to work at Englewood Hospital in Englewood and Pascack Valley Hospital in Westwood too. Like anything, in the beginning, when no one knows you, it's not so easy to be accepted and hit the ground running. My foreign accent remains to this day, and for some people, particularly when starting my career, this was held as a stigma against me.

In order to have a private practice outside of operating and seeing patients at the hospital, I had to rent an office. Without any knowledge and experience in this regard,

Roberta and I found and rented a second-floor office in Paterson, New Jersey. We signed the lease shortly before moving to Teaneck ourselves. The walls of the office had not seen paint in years. Roberta and I would drive from Cherry Hill in South Jersey all the way up north to Paterson to spend the day painting and preparing the office. This took quite a few trips, one day; even my in-laws came to help. This work came at our own financial expense. Little by little, things were completed and my first office was ready.

We moved to Teaneck in July of 1977. Roberta and I purchased our first home. It was a small, Cape-Cod-style home with two bedrooms and two bathrooms. The kitchen was so narrow two adults couldn't squeeze by one another. Although I now realize how small this house was, for us at the time, the house was a castle. It was ours, and we were so proud to be homeowners. So much so that one day we invited over a few older and more established doctors and their respective spouses, only to realize we didn't even have enough space to seat everyone in the small living room. The house's location was ideal, however, as it was about two miles away from Holy Name Hospital. This was especially true early in my career as I was mainly assisting other doctors at this point and not yet having much of a practice of my own. Therefore, I needed to be able to get to the hospital often and very quickly.

When I first started my practice in Teaneck, I spent most of my days in the doctors' lounge waiting to meet other doctors or getting them to notice me in the hope of helping them with their patients and showing them my skill-set. I covered the emergency rooms of several hospitals in order to survive and make ends meet at home. Occasionally a patient admitted through the emergency room would require surgery, and I would receive payment as the operating doctor. I learned, however, that many of these patients were uninsured, so many of the surgeries I performed wound up being pro bono. My first day on call was at St. Joseph's Hospital in Paterson, New Jersey. I was called in by the residents, and from the description and information I got over the phone, I diagnosed the emergency as a ruptured abdominal aneurysm. I gave orders over the phone to prepare the operating room. I quickly got to the hospital, examined the patient, and my diagnosis was correct. The patient was in shock and pale, and we rushed him to the operating room. I saved this patient's life. To the residents and nurses, I was Superman. This was the beginning of my surgical practice that would come to grow over time.

During this time, I was also assisting several doctors in the hospital and also the Chief of Surgery, with whom I became friendly, and he noticed my surgical skills and training. He came to trust my judgment, so much so that he would have me cover his practice whenever he went on vacation or couldn't be available for some reason. In the beginning, other doctors who normally referred cases to the Chief, not knowing me, were reluctant to put their patients in my hands. This was very obvious to me, and although it hurt my feelings, there was nothing I could do but allow time to change this. And as time passed, those other doctors began to notice me as a gifted surgeon, called me for surgical consultations, and referred such patients to me. Although sometimes, as I mentioned before, my accent got in the way, what did help me was the fact that I spoke three languages: Italian, Spanish, and English, and I had a wonderful rapport with the nurses. Years before, I quickly learned to always hold the nurses in high regard and treat them with the utmost respect. The nurses I worked with became my best source of advertisement because they saw firsthand the quality of care I rendered to my patients and the dedication I put into my practice. They saw the very human side of me.

One day when I was covering for the Chief, his secretary called my office stating that a patient was on the surgical floor requiring attention. I went to the hospital and introduced myself. Immediately I could sense the patient was not thrilled with me. I examined the patient and then explained my recommendations. This patient had an inflamed gall bladder and fever, and I recommended surgery. I told the patient to think about what I had said, and after asking if he had any additional questions, I left him so he could decide what to do. The following day I went to check in on this patient. As I walked into the room, several members of the family: his wife, daughter, etc., were all around the bed, waiting for me. He introduced me to his family, and the cold reception from the day before had melted entirely. He was very friendly and polite and asked me, "Dr. Forcina, when are we going to do the surgery?" I was perplexed, given what had transpired the day before, and hadn't expected this sudden change. I excused myself and went to the nurses' station to obtain the consent papers for surgery and inquired as to when we could schedule the surgery. At this juncture, the head nurse and the nurse responsible for his care came over to talk to me. I asked them, "What happened since yesterday?" Apparently, the patient had questioned every nurse and person about me since I had left his room the night before. Given the nurses' wonderful recommendations, he decided to proceed with the surgery and recovered perfectly.

While all this was happening and I was trying to build my practice, my father-in-law had recurrent surgery for rectal cancer. The prognosis was not good, and we were all going through a very difficult time. We all were worried about him. Clement, my father-in-law, was a very meticulous person; this and the cancer made him very depressed, and he was worrying all the time. When he experienced discomfort, he thought that it was the end of his life. As you remember, he had a very great affection for me from the very first day we met. I knew that to him, after God, I was the 'second in command' in his life. Every time we were together, he asked questions, and I always tried to answer the best I could, all the time trying to give him hope, and when he heard my words of reassurance, he was always more relaxed and comfortable.

One day, Roberta gave me the great surprise that we were expecting a baby! Our happiness was immense, and so was the overwhelming excitement of both sets of parents. Upon finding out the great news, my in-laws started to buy toys and would frequently come from South Jersey to visit us. They came as often and as long as my father-in-law's comfort allowed. Roberta was very busy helping me build my practice. Because I couldn't afford to pay anyone regarding office staff, Roberta had given up her teaching career to run my office and help me build the practice. She was a tremendous asset to me. She ran the office and took care of our house, and I was never home and always at work. And, when the time came later that her parents could no longer come to visit us, and when my work didn't allow me to join her, she went alone to Cherry Hill to see them.

Roberta's pregnancy progressed well until one night when she was five months pregnant; she began experiencing cramps and pain. The following morning she was admitted to the hospital for observation. Everything was fine, and she was discharged and sent home with the recommendation to rest. I remember soon after, during another night, while in a deep sleep, I felt shaking and then heard her crying, and with a trembling voice, she told me she was losing the baby. Unfortunately, she was correct. Julianna was born around six months gestation and was less than two pounds. With the medical technology today, her hope and prognosis for survival would be much better, but in 1978 there was little anyone could offer this poor sweet girl who was born too soon. Palliative care was provided to Julianna for the two or three days she lived, and sadly we later had to bury our firstborn daughter.

Those days were followed by moments of depression. I found myself questioning everything, like why did this happen? I prayed a lot for the health of my wife and father-in-law. Looking back, I genuinely do not know how Roberta handled everything. We were young, and on many occasions when we were invited to a party, family reunion, or any social gathering, already having everything planned, as we were leaving the house, the phone would ring, and it was always my answering service trying to reach me for an emergency. There were many times, and frankly, years when Roberta had to resign herself to being alone in the house and being physically away from her; she was a real support and strength to our relationship despite all of its adversities. I thank God for giving me such a companion. I thank her very much for all she has done and gone through and is still doing today.

Thank you, my love. Those beginnings were very difficult for us. We had no experience, no one to give us advice, we made many errors, and on more than one occasion, the tension reached a peak in our lives. As my practice grew, we had to overcome the envy that existed in my profession from some colleagues who resented someone younger walking into their territory. As with anything that will either defeat you or compel you to be glorious, all of this strengthened our intimacy and brought us closer and closer together. This gave us the strength to continue to fight and look forward. It seems like those rough times were a fortifying tonic that gave us the desire and power to confront the uncertainties of our future. I believe all that was possible because being so close produced only one shadow. From that shadow, we got together for warmth and found the strength to fight the desperation and obstacles head-on. Those days do not seem so distant to me. The reality is I can never forget them, for they left a mark on my life. And now, I can appreciate and analyze those times that were so difficult for me.

I should mention it was also during these years when I earned my citizen stripes. I became a United States citizen on April 24, 1978. That day was a momentous and glorious day for me. Despite being born in Italy and living in Argentina for so many years, neither place truly felt like home to me. I was a child when I left Italy, and in Argentina, I had a very difficult time assimilating. It is my understanding that to belong to a place, you need to feel welcomed, and for me, that is what this beautiful country provided. I was filled with tremendous pride to be a legal citizen, have my feet on solid ground, and officially call this place my home. In this great land, no one is considered to be an outsider or 'other.' People are your contemporaries and may have a past themselves, maybe even similar to your own. It's possible that their parents or ancestors also came here with great hopes. That is what I find so special about this country.

For many years I had lived in limbo, with great uncertainty. I was no one in particular and felt like a boat lost in the open sea at the mercy of the wind. Those feelings left me the moment I raised my right hand and pledged my allegiance to

America. The pledge was just the beginning of the promise and honor I undertook, with many bigger things to come. Like most immigrants, I came to this country looking for a better future and to improve my life. To do this, I had to sacrifice many things, including leaving everything and almost everyone I had ever known. I knew I would have to learn a new language here, and although there was fear and it intimidated me, deep inside the odyssey of my twenty-eight years at that point, it remains a glorious day because I saw the potential waiting for me.

Although I originally came to this country as an explorer, as I mentioned before, almost immediately after I arrived, I noticed the immense possibilities this place offered me. I was ready to roll up my sleeves and work very, very hard. It was my honest hard work, and perseverance that allowed me to reach the top. The trick was never to give up during the low moments. Those moments are challenging because your energy seems to leave you as well. Being aware of all this, during those times, the only thing I had left was to ask God to please give me another chance; I wouldn't disappoint him. I kept my promise, and I can proudly say I kept the scale even, appreciating all this country has given to me. In return, I helped many other people, and I was able to restore many of my patients' lives. When my human limitations couldn't produce the miracle needed, I held my scared patients' hands and often gave them a needed hug. I felt it was essential for each person to know they were never alone in facing their adversity.

I believe this country has shown great dignity and respect for many millions of poor souls around the world. Many of these people are poor and sick, and there are times when the United States' aid has helped some of these people have a better life. In general, most people in the world are decent human beings. As with anything, a process should be fair and controlled to maximize protection and opportunity for all. This includes people trying to immigrate to this country and its existing citizens. Those decent humans should be welcomed through an organized process, maintaining integrity for all. Absent this, it's like having a large uncontrolled crowd waiting at a stadium gate, and without an orderly process, a stampede results, and people are injured. The consequence is that what was supposed to be a happy and beneficial time is instead a funeral of mourning for the lack of adherence to common-sense principles.

Like me, I believe honest applicants who are willing to come here legally, to work and improve their lives, contribute to the tax system and follow the laws of the country should be granted admission when possible. Those individuals will hopefully appreciate and live their lives in good conscience here. Doing so will help protect American freedom and contribute to the larger societal well-being. This does not apply to everyone, however, as there are those who wish this country and its occupants harm, and in my humble opinion, I think a vetting process is helpful to weed out such bad seeds.

# Chapter 13
## Vanessa

My father-in-law continued to have ups and down with his battle with cancer. We found out again with great joy that Roberta was pregnant again. However, because of the previous miscarriage, we were very anxious. Roberta was very cautious with her activities around the house. Being an only child, she tried to visit her parents as much as possible. Her pregnancy was progressing well, and each day as I said goodbye leaving for work, I reminded her to call me at any time if there were any problems. One day, she started to bleed around the fifth month of her pregnancy, just like the last time; however, this time, the bleeding stopped, and everything moved forward.

On her actual due date, April 8th (I should mention ironically enough, my birthday is April 7th), there was a very bad storm in our area. Sure enough, as luck would have it, my wife went into labor. She tried to call me, but our phone lines were down. Luckily, we had a key to the neighbor's house, and she was able to get there to call the hospital to have me paged. No response. She then asked the hospital operator to connect her to the operating room but was informed by the surgical front desk I was not there. She then called the telephone company, explaining she was in labor and that she needed our home phone line to work.

Roberta returned to our house and, believe it or not, proceeded to cook some meals and make a sandwich for me to take to the hospital. She got herself and her things together. Thankfully the phone company was concerned and sent a technician to our house within thirty minutes to fix the line. My mother-in-law phoned to ask how Roberta was doing, but not wanting to worry her mother since she had to care for her father, Roberta didn't say she was in labor and that everything was fine. I came home and was very upset as I was not aware of what had been going on. I had been at the hospital during the entire page and never received it! Finally, the hour came when we drove to the hospital, and our beautiful baby girl, Vanessa, was born. I remember when they took our baby to be weighed, I followed everyone around to make sure everything was perfect; she was my treasure. We then phoned her parents to tell them the joyous news. Her father answered, and when she told him the good news, he was so emotional he couldn't talk and had to pass the phone to my mother-in-law.

From that day on, every time they visited, they always brought toys and gifts for Vanessa. Vanessa grew up nicely, and my in-laws were delighted to be part of her life. To my father-in-law, Vanessa was everything. When my daughter brought her to visit him at the College of Performing Arts in Philadelphia, he would proudly let everyone know that she was his granddaughter. When we used to stay at their home in Cherry Hill, he would play the piano for her, and she would run all through the house. Being a very young child and not going up or down steps yet, she loved their house because it was a one-floor ranch-style home. One day, my father-in-law was with my wife and Vanessa at a toy store. Vanessa, even though she was so young, spotted a horse that would rock back and forth on springs. It was bigger than her! She was so excited that, of course, my father-in-law bought her the horse. Vanessa would rock on that horse with such vigor it was very concerning; it was as if she was going to take off, horse and all!

Another time, when my father-in-law was in New York City, he went to FAO Swartz. He bought her another very real-looking horse. It had fur and even a leather saddle, stirrups, and reins and looked like a small pony. To this day, we still have it. He could never seem to do enough for Vanessa. Sadly, his disease progressed, and he passed away just before Vanessa's second birthday. Vanessa was able to light up his life up until the end and filled his last two years with moments of great pleasure.

My parents, sadly, who were in Italy, could not be with Vanessa during her early months. They did come to the United States, though, when Vanessa was about six months old. All I can remember is the joy and fascination of my mother at seeing this baby. Luckily, they would then return on more than one occasion. During one of these visits, it was when we had the rocking horse in our living room. Vanessa would climb onto the horse and begin riding it with such vigor. My poor mother, who had never seen this before and was not used to it, thinking the worst, would stand by, ready to grab Vanessa if she fell. Regardless of our reassurances, she never could quite relax when seeing Vanessa ride her toy.

I was studying for my Medical Surgical Board Certification (Boards) at this time. The Boards is an exam many hospitals require for a doctor to be a member of their staff. For personal reasons, I wanted the academic achievement of passing this exam. To sit for the Boards, you have to be in practice for one year and present the number of surgical cases you have done and managed (this has to be certified by the Chief of Surgery of the hospital where you are a staff member), and letters of good standing must be submitted. The first part of the Boards is a written exam based on broad knowledge and understanding of medicine and surgery. It is a very difficult and intense exam, and, not unlike the FLEX exam, it takes several months to find out if you passed. Only if you pass Part I can you apply, one year later, for the oral exam, Part II. For Part II, you go to another state, and there are three groups of two doctors each who are University specialists well known in various areas of surgical medicine; they question you.

Little Vanessa was never a great sleeper. She woke up at least five times a night. Because I was constantly working and studying for the medical boards whenever I could, my wife would get up and quiet her as quickly as she could. She knew I needed as much rest as possible. At night and on the weekends, Roberta would sit with me and go over questions. She would tutor me on how to reason and eliminate certain answers in multiple-choice scenarios and look for specific words in the analogy part.

The constant studying was very tedious. When I became overwhelmed, I would take a break to do some work around the house. It was fall, and we had a very large oak tree in front of our Teaneck house. The branches hung over our roof, and the leaves would continually drop and accumulate in our gutters. I often went outside to clean these gutters, and I had a big heavy ladder at the time. On one of these occasions, the ladder was uneven, and since I was holding the ladder to prevent it from completely falling over, I overstretched my left arm to support it. I had some minor discomfort but continued on. In the middle of the night, I woke up with a sharp pain in my left arm. Roberta had previously been up with Vanessa, so not wanting to disturb her, I tiptoed downstairs, took some aspirin, and although there was some temporary relief, I became concerned, so I went to the ER and had an EKG done to make sure this left arm pain wasn't because of my heart. Thankfully, all was fine. As the weeks passed, I forgot about this and was reminded of it only when I had occasional shoulder pain, mostly on weekends when I was doing work outside.

As she grew up, Vanessa began to use a little walker with wheels. Nothing gave her more pleasure than to move full speed ahead and bang the door open to the room where I was studying. To help eliminate this and knowing that I needed quiet in order to concentrate, my wife would take our daughter to the park or mall, etc., so I could have most of the day to myself to study. Vanessa grew each day, and her personality formed. We later realized Vanessa's independence and doing things was simply the only way she knew how to be. Vanessa was very close to my wife, and they had a beautiful mother-daughter relationship that grew and continues to grow through their years together. This has always made me very happy because my work schedule didn't allow me to spend quality time with my daughter during her early years. Thank goodness my wife compensated for that.

# Chapter 14
## Building a Building

With time, I learned my judgment in deciding to rent an office in Paterson, NJ, was incorrect. Sadly, the area had declined through the years, and on more than one occasion, the police had to be called. I was concerned for Roberta's safety, as most days, she was there alone. As soon as the lease was up, we moved and rented an office in Teaneck, NJ. Coincidentally, this was also much closer to Holy Name Hospital, one of the hospitals where I worked.

The office space in Teaneck was better. As time passed, I realized there were some parking constraints, and I was also not allowed to display a sign outside on the property, which created confusion for some patients who were visiting the office for the first time and were unfamiliar with its location. I rented this office from a group of other doctors, and as my practice grew, the most significant constraint was the limitations placed on the hours during which I could see patients.

As such, because we needed more freedom and space, my wife and I started to think about buying an old house or property where we could have an office for now, and possibly later, with time and money, fix it up and expand. During this time, I operated on and became friendly with a patient who owned various commercial spaces. This gentleman, also an immigrant, had come to the United States many years before me and managed to create a very nice life and successful career here. One particular weekend while I was making rounds at the hospital, seeing and checking in on all my patients, he noticed I was in a hurry and asked me why I was in such a rush. I explained my situation and told him I had an appointment to see some properties. He then asked me where I was looking, how many parking spaces I needed, and other things. As I mentioned, this patient had become a friend of mine, and knowing city ordinances and restrictions for certain types of offices of which I had no clue, he told me to wait, and as soon as he was discharged and feeling better, he would help me. And he did.

During the patient's recovery, I was able to secure a loan from a bank, and once he was better, he helped me find a small single-floor building that met all zoning regulations. We were very happy owning our new, yet very old, office. It had an office in the front and a space in the back we used for storage and cleaning supplies. In the front of the building was a large tree whose branches extended over the roof, and the leaves would fall and clog our old gutters. When it rained, the water would come inside the office, soaking the carpets and making the office smell like mildew. As the years passed and my practice continued to expand, we contemplated building a second floor above. To do so, we considered buying the old house next door to expand the footprint of the building and its parking.

I went back to my friend and former patient, asking if he could please negotiate the sale of this old house for us. I asked him to do this on our behalf because in the past, on more than one occasion, the current owner gave my office staff an unnecessarily hard time about nothing, and I knew if the owner discovered our intentions to buy his home to expand our office building he would needlessly jack up the price. He agreed to the sale with my friend, and on the closing day, my friend, who technically purchased the property with our money, transferred the title into our name.

After many months of planning and obtaining permits, our engineer, the uncle of my cousin's husband, selected and hired a builder for us. We obtained a commercial loan, and every month, the bank would send an inspector, at our expense of five hundred dollars per visit (this was in the very early 1980s), to inspect any recent work and then, if acceptable, release the money for such work done which we would then give to the builder. About halfway into the construction of the building, we noticed the number of workers on the job site dwindling and inquired as to what was going on. It turned out that the builder had not paid the subcontractors in months! It took some time to figure out what was going on, but we finally did, and the builder had been using our money to pay other subcontractors on other job sites unrelated to ours for past monies owed. Our problems worsened daily when the subcontractors, who were owed money, began filing liens against our property, with more than twenty liens placed against the building at one time. This wound up in litigation, and I was forced to hire a lawyer. After multiple meetings, I decided I couldn't deal with the situation any longer. Against the advice of everyone, even after I was told I couldn't legally do so, I didn't care and fired every single remaining person from the job site. It seemed to me that the law was favoring the wrong party.

Although I rid myself of the builder, my office space was a nightmare. No one was able to park in the back; inconveniences that were initially supposed to last a few weeks went on for more than a year. I had no choice but to hire another company to complete the building and finish the parking area. The new company was very nice and seemed to feel bad about our situation. Unfortunately, they had to remedy many discrepancies of the former builder, so the project turned out costing quite a bit more than it should have if everything had been done properly the first time around. This entire situation caused tremendous aggravation and tension for my wife and me. Vanessa was only a toddler at the time, which didn't make the situation any easier to deal with, as she needed constant supervision and attention. This was a great learning experience in our lives but, unfortunately, not the last.

# Chapter 15
# My Practice and Being a Dad

The months and years were passing by, and the responsibilities of my work were ever-increasing. Besides the surgeries my office scheduled for me every day, there were unexpected emergencies. In order to tend to these emergencies, I had to be available all the time. On more than one occasion, because of an emergency consultation or procedure, I had to postpone or cancel my scheduled office hours for that day. At the time, most patients understood, but of course, occasionally, there was a patient or two who were not happy to accept this change and gave my office a hard time. I understood this feeling of annoyance because some patients had to leave early from work or take time off to make the appointment at my office. Generally, though, a life decision was made in those moments; therefore, that patient was attended to immediately.

As any preoccupied parent trying to multitask, one day, when Vanessa was a young girl of four years old, attending Montessori school in Teaneck, New Jersey, I had an unusual free hour, and to spend some time with her, I decided I would drive her to school that day. We arrived and were parked in the parking lot and always being chatty; Vanessa and I were talking about something when all of a sudden we were interrupted by a gentle knock on the passenger side window. I lowered the window, and one of the teachers who worked at the school informed us, in a worried voice, that she had received a call from the police to tell her my wife had been involved in a car accident. This teacher mentioned the location, and without thinking, I automatically started the car, not even leaving Vanessa at school, and sped away in the wrong direction. I was thinking the worst, and at that moment, my young daughter said, "Daddy, you are going in the wrong direction." Sure enough, she was right. I guess my mind blanked out. Thank God for Vanessa. The accident turned out to be nothing serious.

The years of having a child in our home passed so quickly. One day I turned around, and my once babbling baby was a young woman going off to college. Vanessa chose to attend a college in Pennsylvania. My wife and I both had a lot of anxiety and worry about Vanessa leaving and being off on her own, especially with her being our only child. Coming from such a different background and largely ignorant of college life in the United States, coupled with my daily work, this became an added source of preoccupation that tilted the scale in the direction of things unknown to me. Because of this and being prepared to confront another separation, I had a very difficult time.

I arranged to take the day off as the day of Vanessa's departure grew close. The day arrived, and my wife and I drove Vanessa to her new college and home, where she was going to start her new life preparing for her future. Upon our arrival, I immediately noticed there were people all over the place. I was not used to this kind of pandemonium. There was noise and business, and already one could see the formation of different social groups. I was worried for Vanessa.

Vanessa was assigned to a dorm room on the third floor of an all-girls dorm with two additional roommates. We knew there was no air conditioning, so we had planned ahead and brought a window air conditioner that I could install; I was glad I was able to do this for the girls. The moment came for Roberta and me to leave and head back home, and like all separations, I felt like my soul was half broken. Because of my past experiences and the many times I'd had to say goodbye to my family, the separation leaves you feeling, for some time, like life has no meaning without the person you miss so much being close by.

Our home experienced hours and days of sadness. A dog, Coco, came into our lives unexpectedly (more on that later), yet there remained an emptiness that even Coco's presence could not fill. My wife was in constant contact with Vanessa throughout the day. Whenever I returned home from work at night, I was always anxious to speak to our daughter as I looked forward to hearing from her all day. Many times, however, when I finally talked to her, I noticed I had a terrible time hearing her with all of the surrounding noise and a loud television playing in the background. Being unable to enjoy our conversation, I asked Vanessa to lower the TV; quietly she let me know her two roommates never seemed to leave the room and were constantly there with their boyfriends, neither of whom attended the college. I asked how she was sleeping and where she was able to dress. She said she was changing in the communal bathrooms across the hall. Unfortunately, this brought me even less peace of mind.

As I mentioned, I was not and remain largely unfamiliar with college life. However, I assumed that, like all in life, dorm life would have a balance, and roommates would have common respect for one another. Instead, Vanessa was sharing one small room with not only her two roommates but also their boyfriends, and all four seemed to be in bed all day and up all night watching TV. This took a toll on Vanessa. Although Vanessa has always been very social and likes to have a good time, she has always been a conscientious student, and I knew she couldn't find comfort or study at her own space. I was furious, and before I heard another word, I insisted on returning to the college to meet with the dean. To me, this was unacceptable.

I met with the dean, who seemed to suggest this was the regular life of many students. I was in shock. I couldn't understand how two students who didn't attend the school were effectively living in an all-girls dorm and a room my wife and I were paying room and board for. This new reality was something I did not expect, and because of my naive thinking, I really thought American college life would be more organized. I thought more rules would be followed, and people would have common sense. I thought people went to college to better their future; after all, many parents spend a lot of money to provide for their children's education, and all these occurrences were incomprehensible to me. I was not pleased, and quite frankly, I was angry about it.

Although I had been in this country for many years by this point, this new world of my daughter was a unique experience for me that even today, after many years, when I think and see what is occurring on many college and university campuses, I often ask what students are getting in return for all the money spent. This doesn't make me happy because even a parrot can be taught to pronounce a few words, but that doesn't mean the parrot is using reason when confronted with a situation or a decision to make. Vanessa wound up leaving this school mid-semester and drove there every day to finish out her first college semester. After that, she transferred to another college in Manhattan, where she was very happy and was able to live a balanced life of studying and being social.

Vanessa, always a logical creature, did very well in school, and with my wife's help, she was at the top of her class throughout her academic career. Vanessa was attending her second college and living in NYC on September 11th, 2001, the day terrorists attacked NYC and America's freedom and way of life. Unfortunately, we could not reach Vanessa and she was unable to contact us, which was incredibly terrifying. Vanessa was able to email her boyfriend at the time, though, who happened to be working in Frankfurt, Germany, and asked if he could please continue trying to reach us to let us know she was okay. He managed to get hold of us sometime later; this was, needless to say, a relief beyond all measure. Sadly, the father of someone Vanessa was and still is close to lost his life that day, like many innocent victims of this unnecessary tragedy. It was and remains a very sad day for all of us. Vanessa could not get out of the city for several days, but at least we knew she was safe.

Roberta and I had been looking and were interested in buying an apartment in NYC for about eighteen months at that time, and I had been hemming and hawing back and forth. Finally, I decided that week, after seeing how everyone banded together and how strong the city truly was, that I would go forward with the transaction. I felt inspired to become a greater part of this city and part of the message of not backing down from this attack and only becoming stronger. We closed on this condominium several months later, and Vanessa lived there for many years.

After graduating from college and living in New York, Vanessa often came to visit Roberta and me at our home in New Jersey. Vanessa was working as an executive assistant despite having graduated with an undergraduate business degree. I noticed she was unhappy and seemed unfulfilled. We sat down and had a father-daughter conversation. I asked her what did she want to do in life. Vanessa has always been an ambitious, intelligent person and likes challenges and improving her life. She told me she would like to continue studying. Vanessa is articulate and has a way with words, so we discussed the possibility of her studying law. Since she was a young child, Vanessa has distinguished herself as a leader. She almost always played with older children and was always the one giving the orders and having everyone follow along. Vanessa has qualities that resemble mine; she is highly conscientious and appreciative. She has seen the sacrifices her mother and I have made for her, the ups and downs of my career, and what I have accomplished.

Almost as a direct result of this, she was very concerned that she would not succeed on her own and, consequently, what I would think of her. This never occurred to me, and it was only brought to my attention by my wife years later. During her law school career, she also had, like most students, ups and downs, and because she is a sensitive person, her frustration and disappointment was evident at various junctures. Many times, upon arriving home after a long day, I noticed my wife would be talking on the phone for a long time, the intensity of her voice becoming a whisper, and I assumed that something was going on, but with so many things going through my mind it never occurred to me what was truly happening. I also had total trust and faith in my wife to handle it, as she had for more than two decades.

On more than one occasion, Vanessa was ready to quit. Many years after Vanessa graduated and was employed in New York City, my wife revealed to me the difficult times Vanessa had had, and because she was so focused on her career and her desire to succeed when things were not going her way, she became tense and was not able to sleep at night and was miserable. I was so exhausted I didn't even realize that sometimes my wife had been driving to the city during these nights to spend hours talking to Vanessa and returning early in the morning to our home. I would notice my wife wore a different expression, although again, I was off running to the hospital to operate and prepare for all the patients of that day, so it never dawned on me that this expression had to do with my daughter. According to my wife, Vanessa would ask, "What is Dad going to say if I cannot pass the exam? What will he think of me?" All this was unknown to me, and if I had known, perhaps I would or could have had more conversations with her, and I would have hugged her many more times. I believe her inherited DNA cannot be changed. My wife saw and understood the pressures my practice produced in my everyday life, and because of that, she was kind enough to face Vanessa's hardships by herself.

Vanessa finished law school and began preparing for the New York bar exam. This is a very difficult exam. She prepared for those exams and constantly studied. We were all, of course, worried and anxious about the results of the exam. Not unlike waiting for my own exam results after coming to this country, the bar exam results are released only after many weeks of waiting. During law school, one professor commented to Vanessa that she wouldn't pass the exam the first time around, and of course, like adding powder to the fire, this weighed on her during this time. I could not understand how a person could be so mean even if it was perhaps intended as a joke. A professor should be aware of the anxiety this could cause and provide more stimulation and support, not such words of discouragement.

The night before the exam results were posted, Vanessa came to visit Roberta and me at home. She was very anxious and didn't know what she would do if she didn't pass. In the meantime, I had been going through some papers in my library, and as luck would have it, I came across a letter I had written many years before when I came to this country and was waiting for my exam results. I was going through a difficult time and had to pass my exams that would dictate if I could start my specialization in surgery. I didn't remember doing so, but apparently, I had jotted down my feelings of desperation and fear in a letter that I kept for myself. So I went to get this letter and read it to my daughter.

It was amazing how Vanessa's situation mirrored my own so many years before. She didn't know if she would make it and what her future would hold. I had written so many years ago that although everything looked bleak, one day, the sun would shine for me. I did not know when and how, but I knew inside myself, even all those years ago, I had the strength to fight, and no matter what or how long, I would succeed. This letter was the best medication for Vanessa's soul. She calmed down; we embraced and shared a nice bottle of wine. The following day I had to be in the operating room early for a scheduled procedure on a patient of mine. Upon arriving at the hospital, the first thing I did was tell the nurses at the front desk of the operating room I was expecting a very important call from my wife regarding my daughter's exam. I asked them to let me know as soon as she called. As I was performing the surgery, my thoughts were flying back and forth to my daughter and her emotions and anxieties, which were in some way mine. Finally, my wife called, and the nurses notified me that Vanessa had passed! They congratulated me, and we all embraced like children on a playground.

I have learned, through all these experiences, that the beauty of life, despite all adversities, is that one never has to give up because sooner or later, the right path will be in front of us. Sometimes when my wife, Vanessa, and I are all together, and she has some problem in her life, I remind her of the past and what she has gone through, and how she has already overcome all those situations. I remind her she will overcome new difficulties in her life just like she has overcome those in her past.

# Chapter 16
# My Career

If someone were to ask me to describe my overall career in one analogy, I would characterize it as sunny days with distant clouds. Overall, my practice, although grueling, was enjoyable and successful. I loved what I did, and the appreciation I received from many of my patients and their families gave me great satisfaction. Although I became a successful surgeon, I didn't run my office or schedule my procedures like a business machine. I believed that, ultimately, my success was a direct result of always doing the best I could for the people I was caring for. This, and my skill-set, set me apart from some of my other colleagues throughout different points in my career. The clouds I refer to were the darker moments that caused me pain and sometimes tortured my family. Because of my strict upbringing and schooling experience, I guess I was still somewhat naive during my younger years and wasn't prepared for certain doctors whose principles and values opposed mine and who used arrogance and intimidation in the hopes of monetary upswings.

As in any profession or job, breaking bad news to someone, in this case, a patient, and sometimes that patient's family is never easy and never came, personally speaking, without my own feelings of sorrow for such patient or family. As a surgeon or any doctor, there are sometimes limitations as to what can be done, and not every person can be saved, cured, or made entirely whole again. As a sensitive person who cared greatly for all my patients, I often suffered along with them. As a surgeon and doctor, like anyone else, I was limited as to what I could do by the state, health, and extent of my patients' injuries or illnesses, and I had to do the best with the circumstances presented to me.

I always tried, as best as possible, to explain in the most simple terms what any procedure would entail and any additional possibilities once the patient was on the operating table. There was always a fine line between making someone aware of all the risks and possibilities and not trying to scare them since, in most cases, most procedures end up fine and without complications. I never wanted to create any false hopes, especially for certain patients whose procedures were to extend life but whose lives were ending in the foreseeable future. To me, there was no greater joy than finishing a procedure and going back to the waiting room to see a patient's family and inform them the procedure went well, and although they would need to spend a few days recovering, life would otherwise resume as normal.

Since the beginning of my practice, I had always gone to see every one of my patients before they were discharged from the hospital. I would also phone their home later that night to check in, making sure everything was okay, and the next morning, before starting my new cases in the operating room for that day, again, I would phone such patients. I did this to make sure everything was all right and to clarify any possible issues or instructions that had been given and were perhaps unclear or misunderstood. I did this because, as you know, I have always cared about my patients a lot, and knowing all was well or if some additional instructions were needed; I felt better being able to address this. From my earliest days, my patients knew their treating physician was a human being with a heart. On more than one occasion, when I would travel to Italy to visit my parents, the covering doctors, because of having their own methods, would handle things differently, and sometimes my patients would mention something to my office, usually in disappointment.

At my peak, I was doing approximately five hundred major cases a year. This didn't include any minor issues such as skin lesions, growths, basal cell cancer excisions, and the removal of lipomas, cysts, and other such growths. This also didn't include any cases during which I was asked to assist my colleagues or as the Chief. As the years passed, I realized I was spending too much time running back and forth between all the different hospitals I was working at, so I condensed my practice and focused primarily on the patients I was receiving at Holy Name Hospital and Valley Hospital.

After several years I became Chief of Surgery at Holy Name Hospital in Teaneck, NJ. I remained in this position for two terms of three years each (which is the maximum allowed). It made me happy and satisfied to be admired and respected by my colleagues. In the position of Chief of Surgery, there are many responsibilities. One of the responsibilities is being an arbitrator or judge to settle any dispute between two or more doctors. As the Chief, you are in the middle of their conflict. Another job of the Chief is to assign various doctors to cover the emergency room by being on call. This means such doctors must be available to receive phone calls and possibly come into the hospital should the need arise. It's not an easy job convincing established doctors who have their own practices to take all kinds of calls and cases, particularly sometimes when little or no payment will be received.

I continued to grow and expand my practice for more than forty years. Always being confident in my training, maintaining my training for any new technologies, and being calm under pressure helped me become the qualified and responsible surgeon I was. I feel privileged to have met and treated so many wonderful people and to have been a part of some of their families and life. I retired in July 2012. I was seventy-two years old. During the last ten years of my career, I was also the Chief at Meadowlands Hospital in Secaucus, New Jersey. There are highs and lows to anyone's career, and here are a handful of memories and lifelong lessons from mine:

THE CAR ACCIDENT: Immediately after joining the hospital staff at Holy Name Hospital, one of the requirements was to take emergency room calls related to one's specialty, so I did. During those early years, I saw and treated many situations with favorable outcomes and some with sad consequences. I recall being called into the emergency room one night to treat the survivors of four young adults who were involved in a serious car accident. It rained that particular night to the point some streets were flooded, and the fog made it difficult to see. The kids had graduated only a few hours beforehand and were returning home from New York City when the driver of the car, trying to make a turn and exit the main road, ended up driving the vehicle into a column. Horribly, the sudden impact instantly killed the backseat passengers. The front passenger, a girl, suffered massive internal injuries to her organs and multiple fractures of her pelvic bones. All attempts were made to try to stabilize her critical situation, but despite everything, her injuries were too severe, and she died in the emergency room.

The driver was in a coma but stable. After multiple consultations with other specialists, he was admitted to the Intensive Care Unit (ICU), where he was connected to a respirator and was constantly monitored. I followed this patient for many weeks, although his condition remained the same, and there was no response or, sadly, any signs of any improvement. What I did notice was the constant presence of this young man's father, almost paralyzed with fear, at his son's bedside, desperately waiting for his son to wake up and give him his first hug. Whenever I spoke with this boy's father, he was anxious for information about his son's situation and looking for some comfort. I tried to offer him whatever consolation and facts I could, and we hoped for the best and prayed together. Finally, after many, many weeks of seeing this stagnant and sad scene, one day, I came by to discover the father smiling and much happier than usual. He immediately informed me one of his son's fingers had produced a very small movement the day before. I examined his son and, not noticing any changes, consulted with the nurses in charge of the patient. They all said the same thing; nothing had changed in this patient's status. Incredulously though, very slowly, this patient started to recover, and one day I witnessed his discharge from the hospital.

Although this patient suffered some speech problems, according to a nurse who saw and spoke with him when he came to visit the hospital to thank everyone who had taken care of him, he was able to continue his studies. Fear and frustration can destroy hopes, especially in a bad situation like this. I give tremendous credit to this boy's father, who was so confident his son would open his eyes again one day and look at him and say, "Hi, Dad."

A PAIN IN THE ARSE: One day after finishing several surgical cases, a referring doctor in the emergency room called me to see a patient who was suffering from severe pain from very large, protruding hemorrhoids. I examined the patient and recommended surgery. She had a lot of swelling, and clots had developed because the circulation to these veins was compromised. I explained the procedure and any potential complications. She elected to proceed with the surgery, and it went fine and as expected. After surgery, it is common to be in some pain from the procedure and having one's arms in a certain position on the operating table. This patient, as almost all are, was given prescribed narcotic medication to control her post-surgical pain. She was discharged with instructions and told to come to see me the following week in my office. This is customary, and I always told my patients to call me in the interim should there be any issues or questions. One of the side effects of any prescribed narcotic pain medicine is it can relax the bowel and cause constipation. Of course, diet can impact this as well. In any event, this patient became constipated and terrified to go to the bathroom. During her office visit with me, she claimed her constipation resulted from something going wrong during the surgery and was now even worse off than before. I explained the pain medication was not helping the constipation and tried to assure her there were no issues with her surgery.

She was unhappy with this and decided to see another doctor for a second opinion. The doctor she chose to see was someone who was not particularly fond of me; he worked at several local hospitals, and we had had several prior disagreements over his covering the emergency room at one of the hospitals where I was the Chief of Surgery.

This second doctor said I had made an error in not performing a sphincterotomy (partial cut of the muscle ring that controls the exit of stool) during the initial surgery. Although sometimes these two procedures may be performed together, this was not appropriate in this patient's case. A sphincterotomy should not have been performed in an emergency like this because the tissue was already very swollen, and the veins had clots. The surgery I performed was to relieve pressure and make it better. A sphincterotomy is done on an elective basis (not in an emergency) when there is a chronic fissure, which is dictated by three components: hypertrophy of papilla, chronic cut, and hanging skin tag. The patient did not have any of the three, let alone all three components; therefore, it would have been improper to perform this second procedure on the patient during the initial surgery. Additionally, when a sphincterotomy is performed, there is always the risk of fecal incontinence.

Needless to say, this patient believed the second doctor and elected to have him perform the second procedure. Afterward, she alleged she became incontinent. She returned to me, and I told her I disagreed with her decision to have this second procedure. She was not happy. She left and sometime later sent me a letter saying she recognized I was a good doctor, but since she now had a problem, I should financially compensate her.

A lawyer was provided by the holder of my medical malpractice insurance, with whom I formed a friendly relationship. She saw my pain and, on more than one occasion, suggested I offer this patient some money to end this battle. I grew up poor but with dignity and knew I had done nothing wrong. I couldn't go against my principle of fairness and said no to this each time it was brought up. I treated this patient exactly as I would have if she had come from my private practice and had done nothing different in her surgery than in any other similar case. This case dragged on for more than four years. Every time a letter came from her lawyer's office, I grew annoyed and anxious and could not sleep at night. As the years dragged on, even my wife, after speaking to my attorney one day, suggested I throw in the towel and settle, saying this is one of the reasons you pay for insurance. I was even informed if we went to court, not to be naive, that some people might hold my foreign accent against me or the prejudices some might have against a successful doctor. As you all know, having always been a fighter, I worked very hard to get to this country and become a doctor, so I wasn't afraid of the hard work of this trial.

I won't lie. I was jarred by the fact that if I was found guilty and the verdict exceeded my malpractice coverage, I would be personally responsible for the difference, and I might have to borrow money to pay the judgment. Many days before the trial, I was on my knees, begging God for help. As the court day approached, my anxiety was horrible, and I shook like a leaf. On the day of the trial, I noticed my former patient and her husband dressed as I had never seen them. I also noticed their expert, the other doctor, was not present. He never showed up during the entire trial. When it was my turn to be questioned, I was asked why I didn't perform the second procedure at the same time as the initial surgery. Among the reasons I stated above, I mentioned if this other doctor had so-called knowledge of my 'wrongdoing' in not performing the second procedure that he later performed, why was he not in court to present this point.

During lunch recess, I was unable to eat. I went for a walk outside and found myself dwelling on what would happen if I was found guilty. What would this do to my family? In what seemed like an eternity, while my head spun around from lack of rest and my heart raced to the point I felt like my heart was going to come out of my chest, my beeper went off, stating the judge was ready and had a verdict. I ran so fast into the courtroom I only noticed later my shirt was visibly wet with perspiration. My perspiration grew cold, and my body seemed numb, like a statue. To this day, I hardly remember what happened, although, at some point, I became aware of my lawyer congratulating and embracing me.

Slowly, feeling like I was floating and still not aware of anything around me, I walked to my car, closed the door, and leaned over my steering wheel. I began to sob uncontrollably. It was finally over, and I thanked God for keeping me afloat during this miserable situation. It was a horrible ordeal, and it hurt to be accused of wrongdoing when no wrongdoing was done. Unfortunately, sometimes different people have different agendas, and sometimes you can never do enough in another person's eyes.

I don't remember how long it was till I started the car. I slowly drove toward the exit gate, and in doing so, I passed my former patient and her husband talking with their lawyer. They saw me, and I turned away very slowly. I remember feeling shocked, and all the misery flooded back, but I also recall looking at them and not feeling hate, just realizing they had been my adversaries, and my steadfastness to the truth and doing the right thing had allowed me to win.

GALLBLADDER ISSUES: As a doctor, I could only do as much as my patients would allow me to. I could recommend and suggest procedures and treatments, but ultimately, it was up to the individual to decide whether to pursue such options or treatment.

One time, after performing a laparoscopic cholecystectomy (removal of a gallbladder through a small opening), as always, the tissue specimen is removed and sent to the lab for analysis. Unfortunately, in this case, the pathologists informed me the gallbladder specimen contained a small cancer in the gallbladder. I had my office contact the patient and advised that further surgery of the gallbladder bed should be done because of the early stage of cancer. I suggested we do a wide excision at the base of the liver surrounding the bed of the gallbladder, where the gallbladder was previously attached. This was because the gallbladder was attached to the liver bed, and to prevent any microscopic spread of cancer cells, it was advisable to remove and excise that entire area. I should mention that although the first procedure was done laparoscopically, without opening the patient up, the presence of cancer dictated that the patient would now need to be opened up so the liver bed could be removed. I advised her to also seek a second surgeon's opinion if she so desired.

Months passed, and I never heard back or saw this patient. Then, several months later, this patient came to my office. Sadly, she was being supported by someone assisting her to walk. She displayed all signs of advanced cancer. I asked her what had happened and why I hadn't heard back from her. She informed me that because of cultural differences, her family took her back to Pakistan to be cared for by the local village healer. I will never know if this person was even a real or licensed doctor in any regard or if any additional surgery or chemotherapy was given or done. This patient was dying in front of my eyes, but there was nothing I could do at this point as the disease had progressed, spreading too far for treatment or surgery. I felt very sorry for her and about this situation. Sometimes it was hard for me to accept my patients' choices or their dismissing the rules after surgery. I had to learn to accept there was only so much I could control.

BREAST CANCER: On another occasion, a woman came to my office because she found a lump in her breast. It was more than a lump, though. She arrived with a copy of her mammogram, and the moment I saw it, I knew she had advanced-stage breast cancer. Her examination confirmed this. This patient came to my office with three small young children and her mother. I tried to explain to her and her mother the prognosis at this point, that there was almost nothing that could be done (as in most cases when cancer has metastasized). It was incredibly difficult, especially because I saw the three small children who would be motherless in a few short months. I will never understand how this young woman, who had had children in the last few years and had likely been around medical professionals, wouldn't have thought to ask, look into or have her breast examined at some point when a lump or two could have been addressed. Assuming she was around medical professionals during her pregnancies, I will never understand how a breast examination wasn't done. She could have lived.

I learned that sometimes people are impressed by big titles or an affiliation with a larger teaching hospital or institution, but that doesn't always make the doctor better, more skilled, or bigger-hearted. Another time during office hours, a patient came for a breast examination, and during that examination, I found two suspicious lumps. I obtained a small sample with a needle; a biopsy. Unfortunately, the lab confirmed my suspicions, and during her follow-up visit, I explained the options available to her and the need for lumpectomy surgery. This is when a wide excision is made to remove any lumps while preserving the breast and removing the lymph nodes in the armpits on the sides of the body where the tumor is present (because tumors travel this way). I told her radiation was needed, and depending on whether the cancer had already reached the lymph nodes, if it had, then she would need chemotherapy too, although this would be decided between her and the oncologist.

This patient stated she would discuss everything with her family and get back to me. A few days later, my office staff notified me this patient had called to apologize, saying she had gone for another opinion in New York City, during which that surgeon confirmed everything I told her, and her family had advised her to have the surgery with the doctor in the city. Unfortunately, after undergoing surgery with this second doctor, she wound up with a bad infection where the lumpectomy was performed. Upon calling the surgeon who performed the lumpectomy, she was told to go to the nearest emergency room to have it taken care of. Instead, she called my office, and I solved her problem. I cleaned the infection, and after a short time, everything was fine.

She went back to NY yet again for chemotherapy, and like other patients who don't have good veins and can't accept chemotherapy the way it's usually administered, a portacath (a small container or reservoir placed beneath the skin. A catheter connects the port to the main vein that goes to the heart delivering the medication) was inserted. This portacath also became infected. Once again, she came back to me, and I removed it. We had to wait until the infection cleared, but this time she had me insert the portacath, and she was able to receive her chemotherapy without further issues. Sometimes it's not the greatest name or diploma from the fancy school that renders you the best treatment.

LAPAROSCOPY: As my practice continued and technology changed, I took classes and started doing quite a few procedures under the general title of advanced laparoscopy. This type of procedure came about after I finished my initial training years before. As the instruments and cameras became more advanced and sophisticated, I continued taking classes and receiving certifications, so I was always using the newest techniques and technology.

This kind of surgery is performed under general anesthesia in which two or three small punctures are made in the abdomen, carbon dioxide gas is pumped into the abdomen, making it expand (allowing space for instruments and their movement), and using special instruments, careful exploration is done, and the surgery is performed. Trocars are small tubes placed in the openings and prevent the carbon dioxide gas from escaping. As I mentioned, because this technology was new at the time, all doctors wishing to perform such procedures had to take special courses to obtain the experience needed. After the certification was obtained, the Chief of each hospital would allow the surgeon to perform such surgery with an assistant surgeon who would supervise until a certain number of cases had been completed. Protocol in the hospital where I worked mandated the assistant actually have experience specific to laparoscopy.

Laparoscopy is an option for certain procedures where one's abdomen used to be cut and opened entirely. Opening a patient is a much easier procedure and takes less time; there is less liability for the surgeon. However, with a large open wound or incision, there is a greater risk of infection. If there is an infection, the patient is at risk for weakness in that area and hernia formation. With this large incision, patients generally have more significant pain and need narcotic pain medicine, preferring to stay in bed all day or for many hours at a time. This can lead to complications like clots in the legs or problems with the lungs. Pain medicine can also cause constipation. There is also a large, visible scar.

Laparoscopy is riskier because it requires a lot of experience and can take longer because of the precision required. I elected to learn and perform laparoscopic cases because laparoscopic cameras offer a better view than the naked eye because of zooming capabilities and the ability to rotate, allowing the surgeon to see the entire abdominal cavity. The risk of infection is significantly reduced because the incisions are approximately three-quarters of an inch, and only a stitch or two is required to close these openings. Post-surgical pain and the need for narcotic painkillers are greatly reduced. Patients are up and walking the same day of surgery and often home that day too. Lastly, in the vanity department, laparoscopy leaves no visible scars.

For example, in the case of perforated appendix, in which there are many abscesses of pus and the patient is very sick. After the appendix was removed, I used to meticulously irrigate the entire abdominal cavity with more than twenty gallons of sterile saline and insert long drains laparoscopically to prevent further pus accumulation or collection. Almost always, the drains were removed within a few days after the surgery, and the patient's three small three-quarter-inch incisions were closed with a subcuticular (plastic) closure.

During my career, I did thousands and thousands of surgical procedures; however, in the last fifteen years of practice, I primarily performed laparoscopic procedures. I acquired a lot of experience, and my patient loved the results. I did, too, because they could go back home to their family on the evening of their surgery.

There are situations when timing can limit your ability to treat someone. On more than one occasion, I had patients come into the ER with pain in their leg. After examination, a blockage was confirmed. A small clot in a narrow location of the artery can cause a blockage, and this prevents proper circulation to the leg. After only a few hours, the leg muscle will die without adequate oxygen, and once the muscle is dead, there is no ability to save the leg. It's a tragic situation to have to explain to a patient and their family that they will need an amputation and lose the limb. Had this patient only come in when the pain started, this situation could have been treated very differently.

Another difficult situation, which has also occurred quite a few times, was when I was performing surgery and unexpectedly discovered the presence of cancer. The type of malignancy and its location dictate how and if this person can be treated. Between daily advances in the world of surgery, chemotherapy, radiation, and immunology, there are increasing hopes and treatment options for cancer patients. However, nothing is a guarantee, and it is always incredibly difficult to have to break the news to a patient that they have cancer when they went into surgery for a completely different reason entirely.

As in any profession, there are those occasions and unexpected incidents that complicate and cause stress in one's personal and professional life as well as their bank account. One year, while my family and I were visiting my parents in Italy, my physician's assistant phoned me to say a car had crashed into our building and was literally sitting in our reception room. Obviously, I was in disbelief and couldn't believe my luck that my office was closed that week. Thank God no one had been sitting in the waiting room during office hours, and my office staff was not present. My office was located in Hackensack, NJ, on a main street and only a few blocks from the highway, Route 4. The street was a busy, two-lane street with one lane of traffic moving in each direction in a commercial area of stores and offices. The front door was destroyed, and there was a tremendous amount of glass, as the entire front of my office was a huge glass panel. The waiting room was also destroyed. As it turned out, a woman visiting the nail salon across the street had put her car in park but left it running with her young child inside. In those days, car seats were primitive at best, and the laws requiring them were nowhere near what they are now. The child was moving around in the car and somehow shifted the car into drive. The vehicle crossed both lanes of the road, untouched until the steel beams of my office space stopped it. Amazingly, the child was unharmed. In those days of constant activity between one thing or another, it was literally never-ending. Perhaps because we were young and ambitious dreamers, it was another page in our hectic daily life, but I could never handle these things now!

MISJUDGMENTS AND NAIVETY: There was a time in my life when one day I was called into a consultation to see a patient who had a large cancer of the left colon. I evaluated this patient in the hospital, rendered my option, and proceeded to operate on the patient. Unfortunately, a very large tumor was found. I did a resection, and the patient was free of his disease. The patient did well and was discharged. As usual, a warm relationship was established during a follow-up visit to the office because I was friendly. As a thank you, this patient and his wife took my wife and me out to dinner, and we formed a friendship. Also, they came to our home on several occasions and even met our daughter, Vanessa.

This gentleman was in the construction business. He was an older, accomplished builder and showed me some of his completed projects. He advised me to invest in one of his projects. He said we could start with a small amount and said if we could advance the money to him, it would be repaid in two weeks. The money was repaid as promised. The second time we invested, the amount was considerably larger. Again, he paid back the money in the time allowed. The third time, he asked if I would be willing to invest in a piece of property that he was going to purchase and build condominiums on. The repayment time would be much longer given the extent of the project, but knowing him to have been responsible and honest in his payback of loans, I agreed. He was supposed to also put one of the condominiums in Vanessa's name. I mentioned this to Vanessa, who was in law school at the time, and she had a fit. She insisted I get everything notarized and in writing and we fought about it. I told my wife to get a bank loan, and we gave the money to the gentlemen with a simple handshake and in good faith as before. He told me he would pay back this money in due time. Needless to say, time went by. Months turned into years. He ended up moving to another state, and we never saw this money again. We sued, and although I secured a judgment, this man wound up having no assets in his name to collect against; however, his daughter wound up with a beautiful home on the West Coast, purchased for almost the same amount of money I had loaned him. Sadly, I imagine this is where my hard-earned money went. I saved this man's life, and he thought nothing of deceiving me as a conman, and I was his fool.

I had very bad days and was depressed because of this. How stupid and naive could I have been? After many years I met another man. To this day, this man and I are very good friends. Talking about our lives and experiences, one day, I mentioned this matter to him. He said, "Sal, have you ever seen the TV show *Greed*?" I had not. So, I started to watch it, and I found myself being one of the characters that had been very well deceived and taken for granted. This was an awful experience for me. In speaking to this man one day, after he had promised so often to pay me back, I told him, "I saved your life, and this is the gratitude you give me?" We all make mistakes, but this one still hurts today because I trusted this person, and I was played for a fool. He also took a nice amount of hard-earned money from my family, and we all know you can never have enough in the bank for a rainy day. I could have used that money in various situations since then.

VACATIONING WITH FRIENDS: Shortly after moving to our first home in Teaneck, Roberta befriended some other mothers and their children at the park at the end of our block. Luckily enough, we enjoyed all of our neighbors and became quite good friends. So much so that we are still in touch and enjoy visiting with them to this day.

A few years into these friendships, because most of our children were skiing already, we decided to take a weeklong ski trip to Canada, and it quickly became an annual thing. We either went during the Christmas or Easter holiday, and we would drive up in a caravan of six to eight cars. In total, with all the kids and adults, there were about thirty of us. It was a long, eight-hour drive. At the time, Roberta and I had a four-cylinder Nissan Stanza. Its maximum speed was eighty miles an hour! The car sometimes had a hard time getting up certain hills, and we were always the last in line, as the car would start to shake as we approached the higher speeds. Often our other friends, with larger and faster cars, would change lanes and pass one another, and on more than one occasion, this was noticed by police patrols, and they wound up getting ticketed. This was never fun as we would all pull over and wait.

We used to drive to Montreal and spend the night. We would wake up early the next day, have breakfast and continue to the resort, Gray Rocks in Saint Jovite. The resort had multiple accommodation options and a vast ski area composed of several mountains. There was a large indoor pool, and the meals were quite well prepared. We adults could really relax because the kids were occupied with one another and their activities.

Whenever our days skiing and having a good time were drawing to a close, the thoughts, realities, and obligations of going back to my work sometimes seemed like waking up to a dreary, rainy day after the forecast of a beautiful, warm, sunny day. When our last day arrived, because it took about eight hours to drive home (and sometimes longer if there was inclement weather), and because of our slow-moving Stanza, we used to leave early so as to hopefully arrive home before bedtime, so everyone was rested for the next day. Roberta and I always alternated driving approximately every two hours.

It was on one of our first trips when we were approaching the border to cross back into the United States. My wife suggested she drive through the border, but I wasn't tired and decided I would continue driving. As luck would have it, my wife was right, and I knew from the moment I said hello to the guard something was wrong. I was asked for my papers. I had bought my American passport, driver's license, Social Security card as well as my medical certification that I always carried in my wallet. Sadly, because of my heavy accent, this border patrol agent was not convinced and asked me for my voter registration card. This is something I have never carried on me, and it never even occurred to me that I would need it for something like this.

I was asked to get out of the car and follow him to the counter where the head officer sat inside. I kept glancing at my watch, realizing this delay would cost us hours. Nothing I said seemed to matter. Roberta was very calm, and she followed me with Vanessa against the agent's objections. I suggested I could call one of the hospitals' operating rooms where I worked, where a colleague or two would certainly be present and could attest to who I was. My wife even mentioned her father, who, although deceased, had served in the military. I have to say, although I was very frustrated, I was not concerned. I was a legal citizen, and so were my wife and daughter. This gentleman was clearly not having a good day, and my accent and I were his scapegoats.

Never have I been so pleased to hear Vanessa cry inconsolably! She was so patient, and then all of a sudden, the waterworks started. It was like the place was on fire all of a sudden. The bare surroundings and her crying seemed to unnerve everyone. At this point, Roberta could no longer control herself either and went straight up to the head agent, saying we were being stopped based on my accent and for no other reason than the original agent's prejudice against me. She said she was calling our lawyer. Perhaps because he realized Roberta was not intimidated or perhaps because he could no longer listen to Vanessa cry, or perhaps because he started to think of the possible consequences if our lawyer became involved, after many hours, he let us go.

We were exhausted, and on our way back home, I had to listen to my wife's sermon about how I should have just let her drive. That lasted for a while, but like everything else, as we got closer to home, our family bond was restored. The story was all the rage at the hospital the next day, and I, too, joined in the laughter this time. Like at the end of an opera, there is always a lesson to learn from each adventure, and this lesson was to listen to my wife. Thank you, my dear.

Another year around Easter time, we arrived and unpacked. We weren't scheduled to ski until the next day, so some of us went to the pool while others napped, and some others went to have drinks around the fire. I kept looking at everyone coming down the slopes and decided I felt like skiing. The temperatures had been very mild this year, as evidenced by a few green patches on the slopes. I remember that on this trip, the machines were constantly blowing snow, night and day.

I warmed up going down the easy slopes a few times and felt good. I decided to follow the better skiers, and in doing so, I underestimated my capacity on the steeper terrain and wound up going over one of those green patches of grass. The slight tug and unexpected slowness of the patch of grass caused an issue and pain in my left leg. My week of skiing was over; I knew it immediately. Thank goodness my ski released itself when I fell; otherwise, my leg would have been broken. I was not able to walk, though. I had to be carried and placed on a gurney to be brought down to the base of the mountain, where my leg was immobilized and placed in a soft cast. After a few days, I was able to get around with a set of crutches.

I had no choice but to resign myself to sitting around the fireplace, reading, and watching everyone ski for the entire week. I didn't have any fun experiences or stories to share with the others at dinner each night. I remember going to bed at night, and Roberta had to help lift my leg because I couldn't. I have always hated sleeping on my back, and the leg injury forced me to, so I was miserable. If I tried to change positions while I slept, a sharp pain awakened me in my quadricep muscles. There was atrophy in only a few short days, and my muscles became weak and visibly smaller.

When we returned home, I went to see an orthopedic friend. He gave me the good news that nothing was broken but that it would take some time to heal, and I wouldn't be able to drive. This was a major issue given my career, so every day Roberta would have to drive me to the hospital where I was still operating as I limped around. Everyone wanted to know why I was limping, and I found myself repeating the same story repeatedly for weeks. With time, my condition normalized, I could walk properly, and my leg grew stronger.

The side effect of this was I no longer wanted to ski. My enjoyment of it had been extinguished because I found myself constantly wondering what would I have done if I had broken my leg? Or worse? I wouldn't be able to work. How would I take care of my family? Roberta would be alone, and Vanessa was still a small child of seven years old. Years later, when Vanessa was a teenager, we took a trip to Vermont because a bunch of kids from her school were going there to ski with their families. She brought another friend along too. The weather was cloudy, and it was cold. I tried to ski but was very stiff and clearly not myself. My wife asked me what was the matter, and I realized it was time to tell her I was done with this sport. It had become something too risky for me and, therefore, unpleasant. I said adios to skiing, and since that time I enjoy seeing the snow in movies or the occasional drink I have with ice cubes.

Rhode Island: Early on in my career, to escape the pressures of work and catch up with my Connecticut cousins, once in a while Roberta, Vanessa, and I would drive and spend a long weekend in Rhode Island, where my cousins had a summer home. The house they had at the time was very small, and between their two children, Vanessa, and us four adults, things could quickly become hairy when the weather didn't permit us to go to the beach or be outside. With time they were able to purchase a new home with lovely views of the beach. It was located at the top of one street at the highest point and offered a beautiful panorama of the water and people enjoying sunny days. Vanessa would spend time with her two older cousins, especially her female cousin, Marie. She was always very sweet to Vanessa and being seven years her senior; Maria was like an older sister who Vanessa always very much looked up to. Nicky and I would go out fishing, and at that time, more than thirty years ago, there was an abundance of fish and mussels to catch and make a wonderful dinner with.

In those days, and coming from a close Italian family who enjoyed a good meal, the ladies would prepare our catch of the day. Homemade sauce was mixed with the mussels we had harvested from the ocean's rocks, and the house would be filled with the sweet aroma of the sauce being prepared in the kitchen. My cousin Antonietta would prepare antipasti between steaming the mussels, with olives and different cheeses with some fresh bread. We would sit outside on their porch, snacking and chatting while enjoying views of the ocean and drinking our wine.

Over the years, a few of our other cousins had also purchased nearby homes and would often come over, so there was a nice gathering of us all. After a while, my cousin, Antonietta, would say, "*La tavola e pronta*" (the meal is ready). The children would run in from washing their hands and, after some fussing, would seat themselves according to their preferences. Those meals shared among our family were very special to me. The pasta sauce alone, as it filled my mouth with flavor and progressed into my stomach, left a satisfaction hard to explain. Even today, as I sit here describing it, my mouth is salivating.

Those occasional weekends spent together as a family were very therapeutic for me, like a refreshing shower in the summertime. They relaxed my mind while teaching the younger generation our values and traditions. We were lucky to have been able to pass on such traditions, as I have come to discover that some families do not have many traditions, and to me, this is like seasoning on food. It completes things.

As I mentioned before, we had a Nissan Stanza at the time, and it was after one of these weekends in Rhode Island, after driving for several hours already; in the middle of nowhere, the Stanza broke down. Both Roberta and I were and remain clueless about cars. It was very late and completely dark, and we were stranded. There were no cell phones or anything of the kind at that time. After discussing whether I should walk down the road to the next service station, not having a clue how many miles it would be, I decided we should wait for a passerby and not leave my wife and daughter alone.

Finally, someone came and noticed us. He said he would stop at the next service station to call help for us. Thank God for this lovely concerned citizen! After some time, a tow truck showed up and placed the car on a flatbed. Roberta and Vanessa stayed in the Stanza on top of the flatbed, and I rode in the one passenger seat available in the tow truck. We arrived home in the wee hours of the morning, tired but safe and very thankful.

Those few days of relaxation, family time, and luck getting home safely will forever remain in our memories. Thank you, Nick and Antoniette.

SAVING MY MOTHER (co-written by my wife, Roberta): At this juncture in my career, I made it a point to visit my parents for about two weeks every year. Often, because Vanessa was in high school, she and Roberta wouldn't be able to accompany me on these visits if they were during the school year. It was during one of these visits with my parents that my mother-in-law became quite ill.

After my father-in-law passed away, Roberta and I, trying to diversify our earning capabilities, bought a condominium in Philadelphia for my mother-in-law, Ida, and her older sister, Lily, to live in. They couldn't and didn't want to maintain the home in Cherry Hill any longer, and it allowed us to own another piece of real estate that would hopefully increase in value over time.

My wife used to call her mother every day. As I mentioned, her sister, Lily, lived with her in the condominium. My mother-in-law was eighty-five at the time but lived a very active life, and her mind was amazing. She used to swim every day in the summer in the building's rooftop pool and played bridge twice a week. In addition, she would walk for miles going to the grocery store or to have her hair and nails done; she loved moving about.

Roberta: One day, I called the apartment to see how my mother was doing. My aunt answered and told me she had gone to the doctor because she had a cold and was not feeling well. I said I would call back again later, which I did. My aunt told me my mother was admitted to Jefferson Memorial Hospital in Philadelphia. Of course, my mother had not called me because she didn't want to upset me. I called the hospital and spoke with my mother. After making arrangements for Vanessa to stay with her friend, I went to Philadelphia to check on my mother. Depending on traffic, this took between two and two-and-a-half hours.

I arrived at the hospital and went to see my mother. She seemed in good spirits, so I asked why she had been admitted. She said some of her blood work was 'off,' and the doctor thought perhaps she had an infection. I asked if she'd had a urine analysis done, and she said no because she could not produce any urine. I said she should be drinking fluids but noticed none had been provided. I thought she should have been catheterized to obtain some urine, so I went to the nurses' station and mentioned this. They said they would take care of it. I left that night to return home since I had to pick up my daughter and thought all would be fine.

I woke up the next morning and called my mother. She was very confused. I knew from the way she was responding she was becoming septic. I called the nurses' station on the floor and asked if they had done the urine analysis. They had not. I asked them to get the doctor and or the chief resident and do the test ASAP. I explained why and asked to be called back the minute the test results were in. I again made arrangements for Vanessa and quickly got ready to head back to the hospital. Before leaving, I quickly grabbed some prepared food and general items to bring to my aunt, who depended on my mother for these matters. Lily was in her mid-eighties and in the beginnings of dementia. She was not accustomed to doing certain things for herself.

As I was walking out of the door, the doctor called, confirming my mother was septic. She was being transferred to the ICU. I immediately headed to the hospital only to find, hours later, my mother was still on the regular floor, very confused, and nothing had been done. I was furious. I literally stormed out of her room and went to the nurses' station, demanding immediate action. One of the residents came, and I spoke to him. I was told she would be taken care of without delay. I quickly ran to the apartment to settle my aunt, speak with her, and then went back to the hospital.

I raced up to the ICU. As I approached my mother's room, one of the doctors came out to tell me they were trying to sedate my mother because she was combative. I suggested I go in; perhaps if she heard my voice, it would calm her. I was told no and to wait in the waiting area. Finally, a doctor came to speak to me. He said they had to intubate my mother and put her in a coma. He then went on to say that because of her age, etc., she may not recover and asked if she had a living will. I said he clearly didn't know my mother and how active she was. I said her age had nothing to do with her condition, and he should know there are many fifty-year-olds in worse health than my mother. I also stated if the hospital had done what they were supposed to do from the start, my mother would not have been in this condition.

I went in to see my mother. She was out cold and had only an IV going. She was absolutely not responsive. I was devastated. I noticed her extremities were very quickly swelling. Sal was scheduled to fly home. I was not able to pick him up since I was at the hospital in Philadelphia, so I asked my neighbor if she could please pick him up at Newark airport and let him know what was going on. I was sitting in the room holding my mother's hand when suddenly my husband walked in. Our kind neighbor had driven him all the way to Philadelphia. He walked in, came over to me, looked at my mother, and hastily walked out of the room.

In complete disbelief, I heard him shouting orders to the nurses and demanding that the doctors treating my mother come to her room immediately. Within ten minutes, they were all there. He quickly told them he was surprised she only had an IV going and no monitors. He said she needed a swan catheter, which was used at that time. He pointed out she was suffering from edema and was filling up with fluids, etc. He stood there, making sure everything was done right away while reviewing all of her records. He quickly discovered my mother had been given a powerful sedative, and the amount was enough to put down an elephant, not a thin, fit, elderly woman.

Over the next few days, my mother slowly started to recover. This was because my husband intervened. When she was a bit better, she was moved to a regular floor, but she mentioned she had back pain. An ultrasound of the kidneys was done, but we were told it was normal. We were trying to get my mother stable enough to have her moved to Holy Name Hospital in Teaneck so Sal could properly care for her and have reliable people looking after her. When she was finally transferred, on arrival, my husband found her soaked in urine and complaining of back pain. My husband ordered another ultrasound and asked a colleague to review the results.

My husband, daughter, and I were at home finishing dinner when the phone rang. I hear my husband telling the nurse to get the OR ready STAT, and he would be right over. The ultrasound revealed a leaking aortic aneurysm, and surgery was needed without delay. My husband asked another colleague to assist and was out of the door. My daughter and I then got ready, and we followed. I remember walking into my mother's room and finding her as calm as could be. She had such faith in my husband and the team he had assembled for her surgery. She had no fear. My mother made it through the surgery and recovered. It was my husband's intervention that saved her life. He was a fighter and cared. My mother loved him so much and had such confidence and respect for him. They had a special relationship.

To my husband, I can only say thank you. Words could never express how grateful I was and still am today for what you did. I know from the day my mother met you she saw something very special. She knew the person you were and would always be. How proud she must have been the day we got engaged. She must be at peace looking down on us from heaven seeing all your accomplishments and what you have provided for Vanessa and me. Our daughter has your determination and drive, your special attributes. And for that, once again, I am thankful. Thank you, thank you, thank you for everything and for choosing me as your wife.

REALITIES AND RISK: During my years of training, I got to know and befriend other residents in other areas of specialty. Although after the training finished, we were physically separated, the relationships formed were not forgotten. At the time of my training, I became particularly friendly with an obstetrician who invited Roberta and me to his wedding, and we had a great time. We were both young and very busy building our respective practices, so we generally kept in touch with each other around the holidays and through cards filling each other in on what was going on with us. At some juncture, we found out our friend had been pricked by a needle while operating, unknowingly contracting hepatitis, and was now suffering from liver failure. He died young, leaving behind his wife and young daughter.

During many vascular surgeries, sometimes multiple blood transfusions may be given to a patient to save their life if they are bleeding. During and after the tens of thousands of surgeries I performed, on more than one occasion, in caring for these patients, I inadvertently punctured myself with a needle. As doctors, there are times we are unaware if a patient is infected with a contagious disease. These needle pricks obviously cause a great deal of stress. I always followed protocol and went to the emergency room to have blood drawn and do any necessary tests. In these moments, as a human being, being young and trying to provide for my family, waiting and praying for the test results to be okay was a huge burden that was hard to shake. I would think about my wife and how she would panic, her father's condition, dealing with her pregnancies, and the surprises of everyday life. I chose at these times to keep things to myself and wait for the results alone. This was not easy, particularly as I continued with daily life and my job, feeling exhausted and in fear that my life may become different very soon.

# Chapter 17
## Coco

One day during my office hours, my nurse notified me Vanessa was on the phone and was asking to speak with me. I was very busy between seeing different patients and those still in the reception room waiting to be seen, but because Vanessa rarely, if ever, phoned during my office hours, I wanted to make sure everything was all right. So I grabbed the phone at the reception desk that could be seen from the reception room. I asked Vanessa if she was OK. She said she was fine but couldn't contact her mother and wanted permission to buy a small dog she was holding in her arms. This was so sudden and unexpected it was like having ice water thrown on you from behind. Vanessa quickly went on to tell me she was in a Kennel Club store where puppies were available for purchase. She said she had been struck by one standing in the corner, shaking and terrified to move.

Vanessa, always being sensitive to others' feelings, had picked up the dog and had been holding and reassuring it for the past ninety minutes until the dog finally stopped trembling. It seems this was when she decided to call Roberta and me. As usual, she had done her research and learned the puppy was already fourteen weeks old and, sadly, as always, if the animals do not find a home within a certain period, then their future is undetermined. Vanessa asked permission to bring this dog home. I was so busy, and my patients were staring at me, so without thinking, I told her she was eighteen now and had to start making certain decisions on her own. I really thought she would take some time to think about the responsibilities of pet ownership, particularly given the fact she was leaving for college in just a few short weeks. I proceeded with my office hours and didn't think anything more about this. Little did I know this unconscious and spontaneous statement of mine would cause much tension and many complaints from my wife for many months to come.

It was summer, so the days were nice and long, but by the time I finished office hours and returned home, it was already dark. As always, I pulled into the driveway and entered the kitchen through the garage. I immediately noticed my wife standing by the sink, motionless, with her back to me. I sensed the tension and greeted her nervously. Vanessa was also in the kitchen, nearly in tears. It was then I noticed a little animal following Vanessa like a shadow. This little thing that required so much attention followed any word or movement Vanessa made. No one could imagine my feelings and the thoughts in my head at that moment.

Honestly not having a clue what to say, I asked what was going on? My wife interrupted her silence, turned around, and said angrily, "You want to know what happened?" Roberta is an animal lover, but while looking at the little dog, she said I should never have told Vanessa to make such a decision. She pointed out how much time and care this puppy would need, and Vanessa was about to leave for college, so the responsibility would be hers. She asked who was planning to tend to the puppy at night and every few hours. To be honest, when I lived in Argentina, I had a dog, but over there, the dogs are left to care for themselves. It never dawned on me to think about any of these things, particularly while seeing patients, and this created tension that lasted for several weeks.

Roberta was desperate to not be saddled with this puppy. She even had a moment where she purposely left out her best shoes and gloves, hoping the puppy would chew them and she could find an excuse to dislike her. However, this puppy, which we named Coco, never put a single tooth on her gloves, shoes, or anything for that matter. The poor thing barely had the courage to get to her food bowl. All Coco wanted was to be with Roberta or Vanessa, and she slept in Vanessa's bed, curled up next to her and under the covers. She trained quickly, in less than two weeks, and was truly an angel. When Vanessa left for school, Roberta became the one to tend to Coco and a real mother to the puppy.

Because Coco was so young and Roberta was still working in the office in the mornings (patients were only present in the afternoon), she would take Coco so she could walk her every few hours, so Coco wouldn't cry if left alone. We put a small bed in the office under Roberta's desk. Coco wasn't like the average puppy that would explore and get into mischief. She was an old soul. The whole time Roberta worked there, Coco would stay in her bed and not disturb anyone or anything. Only when Roberta stood and got her leash did she get up. It was as if she knew she had to prove herself to Roberta. As the years passed, Coco came to have special treats, beds, and foods prepared for her. Coco grew into a beautiful dog with brindle-colored hair and a proportionate body. She was a Boston terrier but looked more like a baby boxer, even as an old lady. She remained timid but was calm and loved our company. We really enjoyed hers too. Coco befriended a few dogs on our block as well as the following block, and they would often come to our house, and all run around in the backyard together. Sometimes, in the summer, they would even line up on the pool steps. It was really a sight to see! Seeing these dogs so free and happy gave me great pleasure, like a bunch of children running and playing without any worries — La vita e bella (Life is beautiful).

Coco ended up going everywhere. In the center of Ridgewood, the town we then lived in, the store owners knew her and often gave her water or a treat. I remember one day, Vanessa dragged me to the mall to buy a birthday or Christmas gift for my wife. I have never enjoyed shopping, so I usually tasked Vanessa with these things. This must have been a special Christmas or birthday because Vanessa insisted that I accompany her, and of course, Coco tagged along. As we arrived and walked through the department store, I was shocked to see and hear people calling and petting Coco, knowing her by name. Coco went around to all the right places where she knew the treats were like a pro. I was in disbelief at the scene of so many people flocking to and knowing my dog.

Many times Roberta and I would go for nice long walks. Coco had short, thin hair, and being hypoallergenic, she would get chilled. It was hard to watch her legs tremble from the cold, so my wife had bought a coat for her during the winter from a local pet store. At that time, there was a store in Ridgewood that made coats for people. My wife would store some of her winter coats there each summer. The owner and his wife loved Coco, and one day seeing Coco's winter jacket, he was extremely displeased. Would you believe, on his own, he made her a coat out of shearling with fur inside?!? Needless to say, Coco wore this coat with great pride, and it kept her very warm. It was almost like she knew how lucky she was to have such a beautiful winter coat. Another time, right before Christmas one year, this same store owner called my wife and said he had a present for Coco. When they arrived at the store, he presented Coco with yet another custom jacket. This one was made from fine waterproof material from Italy and lined with soft fleece. Not only did this jacket keep Coco warm, but also it kept her dry in the rain and snow. How I would have loved to have such luxuries as a child growing up!

During the holidays, we would go to my family in Connecticut. Of course, Coco, being part of the family, would join us too. Coco would share in enjoying some of the food. One of her favorites was roasted chestnuts. She would hear the rustle of the bag from the grocery store and stare when she saw them being prepared for roasting. Once they were done, we had to make sure we opened them up and cooled them off for her immediately.

Another joy of Coco's was chasing rabbits when we would go for walks in the spring and summer. Although she would chase after them with great speed, she would never catch them. She also would chase any cats from our property. We would have birds eating at our bird feeder, and once in a while, we would see a cat nearby. Once Coco spotted the cat, she was off and running and made sure they were off the property.

Then, she would lie down on the other side of the feeder as if she was the birds' protector.

Coco had an amazing ability to sense if a thunderstorm was nearby. She was so fearful of the noise. If we were outside and she sensed this, she would immediately go to the door. Once she heard the rumblings, she would go into our basement, where she shook until the storm was over. We would sit with her so that she was not alone, wrap her in a blanket, and try to console her. We had to give her a mild sedative whenever there was a storm or fireworks. She suffered greatly during these events.

I remember one day, I was suffering from a toothache. I was miserable. I was waiting to go to the dentist's office for a root canal. Coco was with me in the house. I was sitting on the sofa with an ice bag on my face, and Coco sensed my discomfort. She gradually came to me, jumped onto the sofa, and laid beside me with her face on my thigh, staring at me with those tender eyes.

As the years passed, Coco became so intertwined in our lives; we were inseparable. The relationship that started with so much strain became so strong and beautiful in the end. Our union lasted fourteen years and three months. Coco left a great void in our lives when she passed and will forever be missed and treasured. Our initial indifference transformed into a deep love, and Coco's death left a huge vacuum inside us, along with some very melancholy moments. One day while in Florida, Roberta and I received a gift from Vanessa in remembrance of Coco. It was a bamboo plant in the shape of a heart resting in colored stones in a crystal vase. This plant has been with us for over six years and is aptly named Coco. It rests in our sunny, light-filled kitchen, where we have many opportunities to pass it on any given day. Many times I am in the kitchen when I see this plant, and my thoughts drift back to earlier days of our inseparable company. Our plant doesn't require much care, just some water and adoring glances every now and again.

One day I noticed one of the bamboos forming one side of the heart had officially given up on life despite our best efforts to keep it alive. Coco, the plant, now has one side, and sometimes I have thought it's time to get rid of it, but each time something pulls me back, and I resist doing such an awful thing. In life, sometimes small things are of such great value, not necessarily because of the present but because of the past. They signify something precious because they came from the heart. We miss you, Coco.

# Chapter 18
# Bella Mare

Roberta and I decided we would take Vanessa away for a week before law school started so we could spend some time together. As you know, I wasn't often able to spend much quality time with Vanessa because of my work obligations and schedule. We decided to go to the Boca Beach Club. While there, at the age of sixty-three, I had my first massage. This was a surprise from my wife and daughter, and it took me a while to relax. I also took my very first golf lesson.

Vanessa graduated high school from a small private school she attended for the last two years of high school. She remains in touch with many of the friends she made at this school, and at that time, one of the couples we were friendly with, who were the parents of one of Vanessa's friends, had recently relocated to Florida and told us to come to visit while we were there. We did so and were very impressed with the physical and natural beauty and relaxing life of Williams Island, where they had chosen to live. Vanessa's friend's father, Harvey, had a beautiful boat and took us around. Roberta and I fell in love with the area, and Harvey mentioned a new building was going up and told us we should buy a place there too.

The next day, Sunday, we went to the sales center to see the models, and I was very impressed. We were leaving that day, so I told Harvey to tell them to call me. They did, and over the phone, we negotiated the terms, and this became our future home years later, once the construction was completed. In Florida, the apartments are often not finished, only the kitchen and bathrooms are completed, so it's up to the owner to finish off the flooring, etc. This can be difficult because you have to deal with private contractors, sometimes that you don't know, particularly when you are from out of state. Finishing this condo became a tremendous job for my wife because over several years she had to make many, many trips back and forth for meetings with contractors, getting permits, selecting furniture, and getting it delivered.

I was still practicing full-time at this point, and because I didn't have much or any free time, we would go to this condo two or three times a year for about a week each time. Of course, Coco came with us, and in the beginning, when Coco was young, we flew there. Because Coco was a nervous dog, we had to give her a sedative to get her into the carrier to bring her on board with us. On one occasion, after she was sedated and we arrived home, we noticed her lips were blue, and she was hypothermic. Roberta immediately called the vet, and it was a miracle we didn't lose Coco. We were very upset, and from then on, we decided we would drive to Miami. I remember how excited I was to have some free time. We would go to bed early, wake up at midnight, prepare a thermos of coffee and sandwiches, and hit the road by 1 A.M. We were like children and alternated driving every few hours. Eventually, one time I couldn't sleep, and Roberta, seeing me toss and turn, said let's just leave now, and we took off at 9 P.M. that time. We would make this trip in eighteen to twenty hours, only stopping for the occasional bathroom break and grabbing a quick bite, water, and coffee. Depending on the season, sometimes there was rain or snow when leaving or returning to NJ. This always added some time to our trip.

When we arrived at our destination, although I was exhausted, I was so invigorated to breathe in the warm air and not have to carry my beeper or phone. The Bella Mare was beautiful. It was new and exquisite. It had a gym and juice bar that served a light breakfast of coffee, bagels, and fruit, and it even had a private movie theater the residents could rent for their viewing pleasure. It seated about twenty people and featured reclining chairs. The pool was lovely and large and very relaxing.

Across from the building was the Island clubhouse with the spa and island gym, where lunch and dinner could also be had. This gym was significantly more extensive than the building's gym and also offered classes and indoor pools. The island is known for its tennis facilities and lessons, as well as its boating slips and docks. As the years passed, Vanessa had quite a few friends whose parents wound up keeping a boat or a sibling or friend who rented a place on William's Island as well. This worked out very nicely because she always had many social plans and friends to see whenever she came down to visit us.

As I mentioned, it took years to get the apartment finished, between the flooring and all the decorating. I remember one time, specifically, Roberta had to fly down because even though we obtained permits for our flooring, etc. to be installed, when it came time for this, we were informed the building's rulebook required a specific type of insulation to be installed (of course this was more expensive) and thus this had to be tended to and arranged. It was finally done, and we were settled and enjoying ourselves. This was not the case for many of our neighbors, though, as some purchased their apartment months or years after us. We purchased pre-construction; thus, we were often faced with lots of noise and the inconvenience of work being done in other apartments. We made quite a few friends, and I became active in some gym classes, such as spinning. I did notice, however, that our apartment seemed to become dusty quickly despite both Roberta and I being very tidy people and constantly cleaning the apartment. I thought perhaps this would die down as people slowly started to finish off their individual apartments.

At this juncture, we purchased the Bella Mare condominium at the very start of the Florida housing boom. As I mentioned, we negotiated a good price for the unit. At the same time, Roberta and I also purchased a much smaller condo near Biscayne Bay for investment purposes. The apartment was in one of the first buildings of a whole area of downtown Miami that was being completely redone. A huge area of many square miles, once somewhat unsafe and seedy, was now becoming beautiful and remodeled with stores, restaurants, and many high-end buildings. We knew it would be a good investment and planned to rent it. We did this for many years and even used it on one occasion prior to the completion of the Bella Mare. About six to eight months later, our broker advised us of yet another good investment opportunity, and we opted to pursue it. We put a down payment on another investment unit in what would be the premiere building in this burgeoning area; it was pre-construction, and the prices would quickly increase.

As the months turned into a year and then two, the dust issue never resolved itself. I was constantly sneezing and having breathing problems. I began to feel sluggish and always felt like I was climbing a mountain in my gym classes. During my next visit up north, I went to see a pulmonologist friend who diagnosed me with asthma and gave me a bronchodilator inhaler, so I could stop wheezing. I never had asthma in my entire life! I also became increasingly irritated at night when I'd be eating dinner or watching television, I would constantly hear footsteps from the apartment above. After weeks of this, I inquired about it because, from my understanding, the floor insulation we were all required to use should have prevented this. As it turned out, our upstairs neighbor somehow got away with not using the specific insulation, and now my apartment and I were suffering. Between the noise and the cracking that can occur as a building settles (our ceiling started to show some very serious cracks), I looked for a remedy.

In the meantime, the Florida housing market had hit its boom, and the market was saturated with new inventory. New apartments were all over, each one nicer than the next. Foreign and many local buyers had speculated and were allowed to purchase with no or low down payment options, and the stock market imploded. The by-laws at our speculative investment stated that owners would be held responsible for the empty apartment carrying costs past a certain length of time (which I can no longer remember), and the sponsor would no longer be responsible. This was very different from any other condo building Roberta and I had ever been involved in, and the building was huge. We were terrified people wouldn't be able to come up with their funds for closing, and we could potentially lose our shirts covering so many costs. Sadly, we walked away from our deposit and decided to cut our losses. We, too, had become "victims" of the low-document loans and stock market balloon.

Sadly, we had to move on, so Roberta and I got a few opinions and estimates to address the cracks and noise at our apartment at the Bella Mare, even though it wasn't my responsibility to address the noise from above, and I had done my duty to protect my neighbors below from this very issue. We were told to lower our ceilings and add insulation. This particularly annoyed me, given having just walked away from the other apartment and losing our investment, but with seemingly no choice, we elected to have the work done and came back to NJ for the entire scope of the project (one can't be present with the amount of dust and all the furniture being covered). Upon our return, we discovered, to our dismay, that the workers had the air conditioning blazing throughout the entire project with the windows closed, and this caused our air ducts to clog. I called another service technician who cleaned them but said there was only so much cleaning they could do in such a building. My asthma condition worsened. I began to feel like I was dying. We went back up north to visit Vanessa, and I noticed my symptoms began to lessen. This was a relief, but I also realized we needed to move once again. The building was making me sick.

Roberta and I had heard from several residents on the island about a retirement community about an hour north of Orlando called The Villages. So we decided to drive up and look at some of the homes. I was very impressed, and we decided to buy a home, even if we wound up renting it out. We were lucky to sell our condo on William's Island quickly, so we packed up our things.

# Chapter 19
# Across the Atlantic

My parents lived in Argentina for thirty long years. They went there when they were young, hoping for a better life, and made many sacrifices, thinking their dreams and hopes were going to smile on them. Unfortunately, those hopes never materialized. The plants had flowers but never bore fruit. The aftermath of military coups brought instability and corruption, and inflation was astronomically high. My parents often said in a period of only a few months, after working and earning money for thirty years, the value of their money vanished like a castle built of sand close to the sea when high tide rolled in.

As you know, my father grew up with serious educational and financial limitations. As an older, educated man, I can now see how this likely didn't allow him to anticipate the future very well. The war affected him and left everlasting trauma. Between all of this, coupled with his sickness in Argentina that went on for years, his daily work went on without end, yet life never progressed or moved forward either in the sense of things getting better or easier. This caused my father a great deal of frustration.

I remember my mother would say to me, *"Figlio siamo finiti in questa terra sbagliata"* (son, we ended up in the wrong place). As I grew older, continuing to see my mother suffer and their lives have no progress or ease, I had more than one argument with my dad about leaving Argentina. However, I was never able to persuade him. I didn't understand why he would continue this way of being, like a person drowning and exhausted, wasting all their energy swimming upstream.

Even after returning to Italy myself, before coming to the United States, I would send letters telling them to leave Argentina and return to Scauri because, aside from having family there, the summer tourist season brought a boom to the area's economy, especially in comparison to anything in Argentina at that time. It was only during my parent's visit to the United States for my wedding, when my parent's met and spoke to other members of my father's own family, that I was able to break the ice and convince my parents to return to Italy.

I got them airplane tickets, and after some time, with our financial help, my parents were able to go back and build a house on their land. In just a few short years after returning, they were better off.

Through so many years, my parents had the opportunity to visit us in the United States, and we reciprocated by going back to Italy. This was both before Vanessa was born as well as after. My parents were delighted with the new things they saw in this land, and the fact we were close to my father's sister, Guiseppina, delighted them. My mother was always so happy when her family surrounded her. I know she would have done anything to remain here, but unfortunately, my father objected to this. My father had great respect for this country and what it offers but felt it was too much for them to relocate again and adjust to the customs here, particularly without understanding or speaking the language.

In Scauri, my father had all his friends. They often got together to share and discuss their political views and solve the world's problems. Being so particular about food, its taste, and how it was prepared, for my parents and where they live, this was part of the essence of their being. The fruit was harvested from local trees, and everything was very fresh. My father would walk three to four blocks to the shore and meet the fishermen to see what the day's catch was. These were things he wouldn't be able to do here, and although trivial to some, these things were very important and a way of life for him.

During our many visits to Italy throughout the years, we spent many hours all together seeing how my parents prepared different dishes, the love and accuracy of which was an art, and with additional members of the family coming over, we would sit down and enjoy the meals my parents prepared all together. They were, of course, paired with wine my father made. My father would store this wine, sometimes for years, waiting for us, and only bring it out on these occasions, which made everything even more special.

During some of these visits to Italy, Roberta and I would rent a car and travel with Vanessa to different regions in the north and south of Italy. We visited museums and historical sites and places. On occasions when I traveled to see my parents on my own, often when I was alone with my mother, we would talk about the times of my youth, our life in Argentina, and the things we went through. Sometimes remembering and comparing everything to their present life in Scauri brought my mother joy and relief, and other times, I would see the wrinkles and hidden tears wetting my mother's face that was once so young and smooth. I remember her telling me, on more than one occasion, the many sacrifices they made in vain, wasting so many years for the end result of nothing. Sometimes she would say, "Son, please, do not remind me of those difficult times because it makes me very sad." I would always encourage her to open up and say, "Mom, it's okay to talk about it and mourn because this gives us strength to progress in life to compare how we lived before and how it's changed." And my dear mother would say, "Sal, you are right," just to please me. Trying to make her feel better, I would point to pictures she displayed in her kitchen and remind her of her beauty and shiny hair so her spirit could once again be happy. This is the way I remember my mother.

My mother always had a special affection for my wife, Roberta. Because of the language barrier, my mother felt she couldn't adequately express her feelings for Roberta and often wondered what Roberta thought of her. During these visits, I would sit on the balcony with her, and she would ask, "How is Roberta? I am sure she is missing you. I love her very much. I cannot express myself, the affection I have for her, but please tell her how much I love her." She would emphasize, "Please, do not forget to tell her that." When Roberta was able to accompany me on a visit, many times, my mother used to say to me, "Salvatore, please tell Roberta I love her like my daughter." Roberta would then go to hug her, and the Trevi Fountain of tears began to flow. My father would ask my mother why she was crying, to which my dear mother would always start gesturing with her hands and shyly say I don't know. Once my mother was able to talk again, and the tears no longer choked her, she would explain how whenever Roberta was able to visit, she felt bad because even though she was physically next to her, they couldn't properly connect and communicate, and she wanted Roberta to be comfortable and happy during the visit. My father assured her that  moments of happiness don't necessarily need words.

When my wife and I were fortunate enough to become parents, we constantly sent pictures of Vanessa because I knew this would give her such great delight and joy. My mother used to look at those pictures many, many times, like a person who wanted to get something extra by looking at that picture; she saw something no one else could see. Following this, she used to kiss Vanessa's pictures, and looking at me with her tender eyes used to tell me in Italian, "*Ma quella Vanessa, e così bella e così cara*" (Please keep an eye on her, pay attention because she is a treasure). Whenever Roberta and Vanessa visited, this brought immense joy to my parents, and they would go out of their way to please and make everyone feel special.

As Vanessa got older and the responsibilities of school and her extracurricular activities increased, I often traveled alone to see my parents each fall. Roberta and Vanessa understood how important it was for me to spend those days with my parents, especially as they aged and their restrictions were more noticeable. I always appreciated my wife and daughter caring and having this sensibility toward me. October became a very special month because, for many years, it was a release of my daily work and a visit with my parents, who were anxiously waiting for me to arrive. In their eyes, I was someone special, and all the necessary preparations were made, the house walls received a refreshing touch, and the refrigerator was filled to capacity with products they believed I was not able to enjoy in America. My mother would instruct my father to go to particular markets for certain items she knew I enjoyed, and in preparation for my arrival, my sweet mother would visit the local hair salon and have her hair done. I always made sure to compliment her as this was something she never did on any regular basis. You could see her pride and happiness in my noticing, and she would mention the name of her hairdresser. She used to tell me, "*Si questa e la nuova moda* (Yes, this is the new fashion)." This simple act was so beautiful because, despite her age and the arthritis pain that her aged joints gave her, in her mind, she wanted to look young because her American son was coming.

Those days were very special. The house used to see many visitors, many of my parents' friends who wanted to see their doctor son who resided in America, etc. As the days passed by, on more than one occasion, I was able to anticipate my poor mother wanting to ask me something but, perhaps because it was not the right moment or because she thought I came to see them to relax, she kept the conflict in her mind and I could see she was anxious. I would use these occasions to hug her against my chest, and she would cry and ask me, "*Salvatore, mi devi fare il favore* (Salvatore, do me a favor)." My mother would ask me if I could please review a medical report of some friends who saw a professor in some big city. This professor had prescribed a particular diet or something; however, the friend's problem was not solved. Perhaps because they didn't trust this professor or perhaps because they were hoping for some miracle from this American doctor, I would, of course, agree simply to please my mother. She was always so happy and immediately would telephone her friend, who seemed like they had been waiting for this call.

I saw several of my parents' friends; mostly, their cases were not related to my specialty. There were a few cases of advanced varicose veins with venous insufficiency. I would suggest some support stockings to help with the problem, and for these friends of my parents, I was some sort of genius. You have to realize my parents lived in a very small town where people talk and word spreads, so on my daily walk, I started to notice greetings and bending of heads, a tradition that had persisted for centuries, a symbol of respect and appreciation from various townsfolk. After my mother would summon her courage to ask me to see her friends, she was so happy, and when her friends came to her house, she would proudly say, "*Te lo detto, Salvatore ti aiuterà, perché lui e così bravo*" (I told you he was going to help you because he is so kind). Looking back at those days, I realize what a pleasure it was to be able to relieve my mother of her anxiety regarding her friends' problems.

In Scauri, the days at the end of October are generally very pleasant and sunny. I would enjoy lunch with my parents, and then my mother would say, "*Salvatore, riposate* (rest)." I would spend the afternoon enjoying their company and relaxing, away from the stressors of my everyday job back at home, and often take a long walk. My dear mother would give me her blessing as though I was still a young boy advising me to, "*Di fare attenzione!*" (Be careful). I would walk for hours, sometimes over ten miles, alone with my music. In the beginning, I used to carry some cassette tapes, but as the years passed and technology changed, I eventually moved to an iPod. I would walk the hills and small paths made years ago by the daily passing of local animals going to the fields to graze. The small things were constant reminders of different times and people, like me, stepping on the same stones for all different reasons. We all leave our mark. I would allow my thoughts to be free, and in those moments, I found a harmony that suited me. To my ears, the arias and melodies of the music sounded like heaven on earth, and I would thank God for allowing me to appreciate and have such moments.

I would first ascend some hills and end up at a promontory where during the sixteenth or seventeenth-century observation towers were built due to the frequent excursions of the Saracen pirates. I assume they were able to send smoke and flame signals during the day and night respectively, to alert others of incoming danger at that time. Still today, vestiges remain of the old days reminding us of those terrible times. I would pass the bottom of what was once my grandparents' stone house built in the mountains. Years ago, when I visited my aunt, I noticed some changes were made, and to me, it was just a small picture of what was once during the war. When I would reach the plateau of whatever hill I was ascending for that day, I would find and rest on a large stone, sitting on it like a chair. Between the views and my music, I couldn't help but think this wouldn't be a bad place for a soul to find eternal peace. I once told my friend John, an orthopedic surgeon and colleague of mine, I would find great pleasure in using solar energy to charge my iPod to play alternating requiems of Verdi and Mozart in that location for eternity. He, too, was a lover of the classics. That was how much pleasure this place, air, and sounds brought me.

During my walk, I would see Spiaggia Dei Sassolini, which is the beach of the pebble stones where Nino Manfredi, a famous Italian actor, built one of his residences. Also on that beach Per grazie ricevuta was filmed. This movie premiered at the Cannes film festival in 1971. The Count of Montecristo was also filmed there with Gerard Depardieu in 1998. I could see all the lidos stretched along the beach with its beautiful water. I would walk from Monte D'oro up to Monte D'argento.

As I descended from the hills, I was able to admire the landscape below, the beautiful Gulf of Gaeta with the distant, infinite sky touching what seemed to be the end of the horizon, the Appian way below with its history, the legions, the thousands and thousands of visitors who through the centuries were lucky enough to have visited this region. I would see in the big valley below the houses made of material that withstands some measure of seismic occurrences and sometimes notice some new construction by the gardens circling the houses protected by iron fences to keep out any possible troublemaker. I always found it interesting that after so many years of history, the mentality remains of the castle walls still needing to be protected by a moat and big walls. On flat land once again, I would follow a small street to an underpass of the highway above as well as the railroad tracks and pass the old church I previously mentioned that would host the orchestra once a year during my father's youth. I would pass the location of my grandfather's cart accident with the broken wheel that took his life many decades ago, as well as a small street that had the remains of the creek coming from the mountain top where my father's family used to farm and where he hid from the German patrols in the cold water.

When I would get close to home, I would find my mother looking at the street for a sign of my return and ready to alleviate my fatigue with a nice cold glass of orange juice. She would say, *"Propio adesso ho spremute le orange."* (I just squeezed the oranges). It was then we would begin our special conversations. She would ask me, *"Hai fatta la camminatta?"* (Did you take a long walk)? She would then ask me if I had other plans and when I said no, she would very gently take me by the hand and we would go and sit on the balcony together. She would say, *"Facciamo due chiacchiere."* (Let's exchange a few words). And sitting across from one another, I could sense her tension, and very slowly, like a person who has to test the lake water to see how cold it is, I used to try to anticipate what she wanted to talk about that day.

She would ask a lot of questions about Roberta and Vanessa. She always wanted to make sure they were alright and would worry about them. I repeatedly answered her questions more than once, but she was so thirsty for news, it was never enough to satisfy her desires. When she heard all the good news, it was like an elixir that gave her energy and joy. At the end of our conversations, she would advise me to *"Perche ella cosi buono"* (Love my wife) and implore me to please take care of Vanessa. She told me she had beautiful memories of those days they spent together. Like Radames (a character from the opera *Aida* by Verdi), an Egyptian general in charge of the Egyptian army once said, *"Come scordar potrei?"* (How can I forget my land and my parents?). Although the days visiting my parents were very simple, and I moved away many years ago to live a different life, these conversations and memories have left their mark.

I remember one day I told my mother I wanted to leave my footprint on those beautiful sidewalks along the beach, which to my mother, to hear I was happy, made her simple world a paradise and gave her such joy. I can only say those were beautiful days. There was something special about them. I felt myself to be a human being, and I suppose those were the feelings Ulysses had after ten long years when he was able to come home and enjoy his family. Despite the centuries that have passed since Ulysses' time, we had something in common, and that is okay with me. Sometimes today, after so many years have passed, those memories don't seem real and are more like a dream. I try to relive those moments, looking at the many pictures that give testimony to the years I was able to share with my parents.

Often during these visits, my father would ask me to accompany him to attend some business in a public place and considering my father's age, I was more than pleased to help him to navigate a system that was sadly chaotic and disorganized. To the locals, it was a common occurrence to spend hours waiting in line only to be told the director of the bank or post office was unfortunately not in that day and to please return the following Monday when they were expected back. However, to my father, it seemed like I was the only person able to solve his problems because, sadly, as in most socialized countries, there is a deep state of bureaucracy, and for him, I possessed the keys to open that secret door.

As that Monday approached, my father used to remind me ahead of time, saying, "Sal, don't forget on Monday we have a meeting with the Director of the bank, etc." It was clear to me that this weekly obstacle of settling issues of daily life was extremely stressful and created tension in elderly people's lives. Never wanting to disappoint or let down my father, I always assured him of my commitment to whatever case or issue was at hand. We used to go to the bank early before its doors were even open, and to please my father we would have a coffee very close by until my father confirmed that the bank's doors would be opening and we should go. I understood my father's anxiety increasing because, at that very hour, there would already be many people waiting, all having to face the same limitations of a system unfriendly to them. Like a wild horse who has escaped its corral and taken advantage of its freedom, sadly, the system in place didn't seem to have much structure or order, and it was more like a zoo of people.

As the years passed, I did notice some improvements in the system, like when you took a number, il biglietto, from the machine and would then wait to be called. We would sit down if a bench was available, or sometimes a courteous person, seeing my father's advanced age and the deformities of his body posture due to advanced arthritis, felt sorry and would offer their seat until we were called.

My father would first speak with someone he knew, and after half of his problems were solved, he would request to speak with the director. At this point, the messenger would inform the director that Mr. Forcina was present with his son, who was visiting from America. The director would emerge, and because of previous monthly encounters with my father, a cordial hello was exchanged, and after shaking hands, we would be invited into the director's office. Immediately it was as if I was speaking to someone I had known for a long time, and when we started a conversation, the topic always seemed to be about life in America. My father always used to use this moment to make sure the director was aware I was a surgeon in America and the Chief of Surgery etc., and then, as a minor item, did my father feel confident enough to mention his problem to the Director.

After some time thinking, the Director would assure my father that with time, there was not going to be any further problem. For my father, the heavy burden was lifted, and he was pleased and happy. We used to leave the bank, and along our way home, my father used to ask me, "Sal, what do you think of the director?" I would please my dad and make some remark that the gentleman was a nice person. My father was proud because now the director knew Armando Forcina had a son in America who was a surgeon! Upon arriving home, my mother was always anxious to know the outcome of the meeting, and many times as my father walked into the kitchen, without saying a word, my mother could read my father's expression, and this was enough to satisfy her that all was well.

As I would move around the house in the following hours or days, my mother used to ask me in different ways, "Sal, what do you think about the Director?" I would give her a favorable opinion, and she was delighted that I agreed with her, "*Si perché il Direttore e molto gentile*" (Yes, the Director is very kind). My mother would tell me that every time after that when they went to the bank, the director would come out and shake their hands. This was a sign of respect, and I remember during our weekly telephone conversations, my mother would mention, many times, that the Director had sent his regards. This is the environment in which my parents lived their daily lives. In some ways, I compared Scauri, at that time, with the little world of Don Camillo, written years ago by Guareschi. Comparing those two worlds and thinking about the advances the Internet has produced, I felt a big gap had been created. For my parents and the local people, their daily interchanges in the market or street were a natural occurrence; thus, they didn't need something they couldn't understand.

As my parents aged, it was hard to face the daily situations of their lives that needed attention. I could see the tension building, and for them to have someone they trusted at their side gave them a different outlook, and in their minds, the security of having me, their son, who was a doctor in America, made them feel like people who would not be taken lightly. I could see quickly that this in itself was not a common occurrence, and inside myself, I always had ambivalent emotions; I was glad to please them, but at the same time, to me, it seemed that the old Borbonic mentality was still present and kept them subjugated, like being in chains. I always struggled to understand and help the reality of their life, but I could only accomplish so much in a week or two.

Through the years, every time I visited my parents, I noticed how their lives were changing. My father's energy and daily activities were taking their toll. I mentioned to my mother that at some juncture, she would need help to keep the house in order and for some basic daily tasks. She insisted she was fine and did not want to hear a word about it. She told me when, in the future, she no longer had the energy to maintain everything, she would consider it.

Given that my parents were in their eighties and slowly declining, my wife and I decided we would make certain tasks, like laundry, a bit easier by purchasing a washer machine and dryer for them. Believe it or not, my parents had never availed themselves of this technology. So, Roberta and I went to the next town, Formia, and purchased these machines and arranged for delivery within the next week.

When we returned to the house and shared the exciting news with my parents, my mother got very upset. She went on about how it was no big deal for her to hand wash and hang the clothes and why did we waste all this money, etc. I took my mother to the side, and even though I knew Roberta didn't perceive it like this, I told my mother she was refusing to accept Roberta's gift. Immediately, not wanting to offend Roberta, my mother stopped lamenting and hugged Roberta explaining how appreciative she was of the new machines. This is how we had to pacify my parents into accepting help in their lives at times. Eventually, the time did come when further help was needed for basic things like cleaning, helping them cook and clean themselves, and they were fortunate to find a lady from Albania, Linda, who took excellent care of them. I am eternally grateful for all she did for my parents.

At some juncture, my annual visits came to cause me a sense of anxiety because I feared perhaps this visit would be the last time I would see one of them alive. One day, I received the call I had been dreading. I was told my mother had suffered a stroke and was in a coma. She was taken to the hospital in Formia. Roberta made arrangements for me to fly to Scauri. That flight seemed like an eternity. I was convinced I would land and be told she had passed away. I got to the hospital and found my mother had been admitted. I asked Linda what had happened, and she said she noticed my mother was having a stroke and called for an ambulance. When they got to the hospital, because of my mother's state and being nearly dead, she was left in a corner, and for several hours nothing was done. Linda stayed by her side and, after many hours, knowing I would raise hell seeing this, at least got the nurses to start an IV so my poor mother could receive some hydration.

You have to remember that Italy has socialized medicine. In a socialized system, there are limited resources, and they have to be distributed to those most likely to benefit or survive. This generally does not include the elderly or very sick. Sadly, these people are usually left to die in one way or another. My mother was finally admitted to a hospital floor, only to be placed in a room with another patient suffering from pneumonia and coughing constantly. This was the situation when I arrived and went to see my poor mother. The hospital did not have air conditioning, so the windows of the room were open with no screens, and there were flies everywhere. The shared bathrooms were without toilet paper (patients' families had to bring their own), and those patients who could eat had to carry their own soup and trays. This was incomprehensible to me. Linda was even bringing personal linens from my parent's house to keep my mother in clean bedding.

My mother was very frail and unable to eat because of the stroke. Having been filled in by Linda and seeing the immediate surroundings, I was beside myself and enraged. I started to ask questions and was told my mother's IV would be suspended at night and only turned on during the day. I was incredulous because she would receive no nourishment or hydration all night! I was going insane but reminded myself to try to figure something out first. I feared an outburst would jeopardize the very poor and inadequate care my mother was barely even receiving; what if they retaliated against my mother?

I spent those days with my mother in the hospital every day. I continued to be shocked by the things I saw in a first-world country less than one hundred miles from Rome, a major city and the capital of Italy. I felt very bad for my mother and the people in this hospital. In a way, they were intimidated. The patients and their families were waiting all day for the doctor to come. Things typically done in the United States seemed to be a rarity. However, because of my mother's condition, I was forced to try to make the best of the current situation, get her whatever help I could, and get her stable enough to be moved out of there.

One afternoon I left for a short time to have lunch with my dad. Upon returning, it was impossible to park. People seemed to park anywhere; there was no order. I finally found a spot and arrived at my mother's room to find her IV line infiltrated. All of the contents which were supposed to be intravenously hydrating and nourishing her were not; instead, her bed sheet was all wet with the contents of the IV bag.

I went to notify the head person and was told the issue would be addressed. I turned off the IV because it was producing tremendous swelling in my mother's arm. I was pacing back and forth, waiting for someone to come, and when no one came after a few hours, I decided to take care of it myself. I cleaned and fixed my mother's IV and restarted it.

When someone finally did come and saw what I had done, she confronted me. Sadly, it seems that unless someone is very well connected or very rich, no one says anything and accepts the meager care they are given. Well, I'd had enough. The accumulation of what I had seen and all the suppression of my feelings flowed out of me like Niagara Falls. She eventually lowered her head and left the room. I felt better and sorry all at the same time. A doctor came. He was very apologetic, and from that day on, as the nurses slowly found out I was a surgeon in the United States (which is a big deal to this day in Italy), they came to call me "*Il Professore*" (the American doctor) and things changed a bit regarding my mother's care.

Little by little, my mother slowly recuperated. She was paralyzed on one side of her body, and because of that and not being able to rotate in bed, in just a few short days in the hospital, she had developed decubitus ulcers on her back, gluteal area, and on her heels. With proper care, this is preventable. Again, I could not understand how this happens in this day and age. Sadly, again, it's a system of limited resources and nurses. People are left with substandard care. I knew I needed to supervise my mother's care. I called Roberta and had her arrange to ship a special mattress, medicines, and equipment. I then taught Linda how to debride the gangrenous ulcers. Linda did such an excellent job with the debridement that my mother's ulcers were completely healed in a very short time. As my parents got older, I began to visit about every six months because they were in greater need of help, and I wanted to check in on things.

I returned home exhausted and stressed and visibly displaying signs of this. I was miserable and in a bad mood, so my wife suggested we go see our cousins in Rhode Island for a few days. Naturally, I jumped at the opportunity to clear my mind. Within forty-eight hours of arriving there, however, I began to feel very tired, had chills and a fever. I told Roberta we needed to head home, and I went to see a colleague for a chest X-ray. I was diagnosed with pneumonia and placed on antibiotics. While I recovered, I couldn't help but think of my poor mother and what she had gone through and prayed for her to get better. I still couldn't get over the medical system in Italy.

A few months later, when it seemed my mother was almost completely recuperated, she suffered a second stroke, and this time it permanently affected her. My mother lost her ability to speak and eat, and sadly, not long after, she passed away. She was ninety-five years old. Aside from mourning the loss of my mother, my ninety-seven-year-old father was now alone. This caused me tremendous pain and anxiety.

Over the next several years, my father deteriorated. He was no longer able to stand on his own. Although his mind was functioning normally, his body was not cooperating. Until his very last days, he spoke of his youth with such perfect memory it was as if those days were last week. Then, one night in the spring of 2015, while watching a soccer game, he tilted his head and stopped breathing. Linda was there and called me. Oddly enough, Vanessa had just been married and returned from her honeymoon only days before. I went to the funeral and the church. My parents had purchased four plots at the cemetery, all close to each other. In these plots are my mother and father, my mother's closest brother, and his wife.

Life is beautiful when one is young. It is the spring of our lives. Happiness and health generally abound, and there is no realization that this will one day change. But, that springtime passes through the summer into the fall and winter of our lives, and those facts of life announce changes are coming. Life is like turning the pages of a good book. It starts fresh, and life experiences go up and down until the book is closed, withered with some folded and stained pages. You lower your head, and very tenderly, in a whisper, you say, "Mom and Dad, thank you for all you have done for me." Those days were very special for me, and I have fond memories of them. Thinking of my mother, who is now in heaven watching over me, is emotional, but I have a serene sense of nostalgia in remembering her.

I am very grateful my parents lived to see my dreams realized, and all those things that were once so far away became a reality for me. It gives me great happiness and pleasure to, in some way, have been able to change their lives for the better too, and to know they lived their last decade or two having put to bed all the nightmares of the past comforts me. I really miss you, Mom and Dad.

# Chapter 20
# My Dear Friend

As you know from previous chapters, we lived in Ridgewood, NJ, for many years. Adjacent to our house, there was a Tudor supposedly built by two sisters who modeled the home from British architecture. This home was built at the beginning of the twentieth century. At that time, the house was very grand because it compromised all of the land. Many years later, the land was subdivided, and many other homes and roads were built. The house was unique as it now sat sideways between two streets; it was on two plots of land and had an Olympic-size pool.

One day a new family moved into this house. We did not get to know them until one day, they came over to meet us since Vanessa attended the same school as their niece; and where their daughter had previously graduated. I remember hearing the gentleman say he had not necessarily been looking forward to meeting me since I had an accent and he could not figure out where I was from. However, once we met, the ice quickly started to melt.

We chatted and exchanged our backgrounds and accomplishments. I learned he was an avid swimmer. So much so that he kept the outdoor pool heated year-round and swam every day for about an hour to an hour-and-a-half. He kept a daily record of his lap speed, and each day he would pick a year and recall with acute accuracy all the events of each day of that year (this was his own personal board meeting). Clearly, he was exceptionally talented and a genius. He was also an older man, many years my senior, and although I was in my fifties when I met him and had accomplished much on my own, he became a mentor to me.

Slowly but surely, our friendship started to form. I told him everything you now know about me from reading this book, my dreams and hopes, and what I had accomplished so far. I told him what I still hoped to accomplish in my life, career, and family. He came to admire me for what I had gone through and how far I had come to achieve the American dream. Also, he particularly admired my knowledge of history and my common sense. I learned he was an engineer, a graduate of MIT, and his grandparents were Russian Jews. My struggle for survival resonated with him as his grandparents had also struggled, in their early times, to achieve their own degree of prosperity. I was intrigued that he had over two hundred and fifty patents, ran his own company, and truly was a gifted genius.

As the months passed, my office received calls from this friend's secretary, asking if I could join him and a group of the engineers who worked for him for Friday night dinners. I noticed when I was able to do so, he was delighted and had sincere appreciation towards me. This became a weekly routine that went on for many years. On those Friday get-togethers, we went to various restaurants. Mostly we sat in a private room so we could discreetly exchange ideas about history and, sometimes, politics. It's imperative to note my friend and I were polar opposites when it came to politics. As the months progressed and I became more comfortable with being more outspoken, we wound up having quite a few confrontations, but we had great respect for each other, and these always ended with a smile and a handshake. Almost always, I stood alone in my challenges and viewpoint. The others sat and listened. Months later, my dear friend privately told me he admired when I spoke my opinion and beliefs and that I was not afraid to debate with him. He said no one ever did this; sycophants surrounded him.

Our relationship grew, and whenever I was unable to join on a Friday evening, he would call and or come through the fence to visit and let me know he missed my presence.

During our meetings and dinners, and because I was a surgeon, many times people asked me questions and were excited about things I explained since there were times they had read or heard something in the newspaper or on the news and were looking for clarification or more information. I was able to clarify their misconceptions and misunderstandings since I could explain things on a rudimentary level. I got to know the other dinner guests quite well, and we had a nice dialogue over the years. My friend called me one day about an employee of his. The daughter was having some issues, had been seen by her pediatrician, and was referred to a pediatric surgeon. The family was very nervous because the daughter was not getting better and asked if I could please see her. I did so and diagnosed advanced appendicitis. I performed a laparoscopic appendectomy, and she did very well.

A few months later, I received another call. One of the gentlemen dinner attendees called about his daughter as well. She was in her twenties and had been experiencing abdominal attacks, on and off, for many months with fever and indigestion and was not always able to eat. She had seen a gastroenterologist who ordered lab work, and recommendations were made, but there was no improvement. I saw her and ordered a gallbladder ultrasound (which was never done), and her gallbladder was full of stones. I did a laparoscopic cholecystectomy (removal of the gallbladder). She did well and went home the same day. I was treated like royalty at the next Friday night dinner.

One summer day, we were at my friend's house for a barbecue. He was cooking a very large piece of meat on the grill. He was dressed in Bermuda shorts and flip-flops, and as he was bringing the cooked meat into the house, the heat of the platter (it was a foil broil pan) made him unsteady and a small amount of the liquid spilled onto the tile floor. His flip-flop moved through the grease, and he lost his balance and fell. The entire meat platter and its hot juices spilled all over my friend's left leg. He was burned and in a great deal of pain. He refused to go to the emergency room but wanted me to take care of him. I did the preliminary care, and within twenty-four hours, he developed tremendous blisters and second-degree burns over the anterior part of his upper and lower left leg. I treated and saw him at least once, if not two to three times a day. I would debride the dead tissue and apply medication as indicated to prevent infection and help with the pain. As the days passed by and he was getting better, the first thing he asked was when would he be able to swim? At the same time, his wife would take me to the side, asking me to please discourage him from swimming until everything was healed. I did my best for several days until he just couldn't take it any longer, and back in his pool he went. Gradually he got better and was very appreciative.

On another occasion, my friend came to my office. He was in pain, and upon examination, I found that he had a hernia. Although it was reducible, there was a potential for incarceration that would compromise the bowel. I advised him to have surgery that I ended up doing laparoscopically. I discovered during the surgery that he also had another hernia on the opposite side, which I also repaired. As a post-surgical directive, after this type of surgery, I tell my patients to walk a lot and to drink liquids for twenty-four hours. This is so the gas placed inside the belly during laparoscopic surgery is reabsorbed. The mobility of the intestine then also has a chance to return. Of course, my friend did as he pleased. He felt good and ate. However, his abdomen became distended, and he became uncomfortable and constipated. In the middle of the night, he called me. I went through our connecting fence to examine him and found that he had ileus, distention of the abdomen, and paralysis of the intestine. His wife informed me what he had eaten, and I gave him hell. I made him walk back and forth for some time, and the following morning, following all my instructions this time, he began to feel better.

Our families often got together and talked about many different things. One year, as Vanessa and their niece were graduating from high school, we decided to find a trip we could all take together. We decided to take a lovely Mediterranean cruise. The cruise ship was brand new at the time and originated in Istanbul, with stops in Efeso, Athens, Venice, Capri, Monte Carlo, and Barcelona. My friend wanted to fly a certain way and wanted only me to fly with him. So, my wife, her friend, and the children flew and met up with us the following day. At all the ports of call, we went on great excursions. My friend, the avid swimmer, had arranged for a hotel at each place with an Olympic-sized pool so he could do his laps. We all had a great time, enjoyed the food, and the kids danced in the disco suspended over the ocean, and many memories were made.

A few years later, my friend and his family moved a few towns over. Although I didn't see him every day, we kept in touch, and I continued to see him on Friday evenings for dinner. I received a call from his wife one day. She informed me my friend was in trouble. Unknown to me, he had been bleeding and went to a doctor and was told he had stage four colon cancer. They were going to go to New York for a consultation, and my friend wanted me to join them. Treatment was started, and because he had such faith in me, he had all of his doctors send me reports of all his test results, etc.

I would talk to both the doctors in New York and New Jersey and then speak to him. Those moments were very sad for me because although we all knew the final outcome, I had to give him as much hope as possible despite all of his questions and fears. As the months passed, the disease progressed, and his condition worsened. He told me I was his quarterback and wanted me by him as much as possible to once again answer all his questions. My family and I were with him and his family the day before he passed. I lost a great friend. Knowing we would never share those Friday nights again, have our goodhearted talks and no longer enjoy each other's company was a very hard thing for me to accept. Sometimes, before I moved to Florida, depending on traffic, I would purposely take the road passing the cemetery where he is buried. Each time I would go by, I would allow the memories to flood my mind, and I would say hello to my friend and then say a prayer. Rest in peace, my dear friend.

# Chapter 21
# Time Together

HURRICANE SANDY (SANDY): On October 22, 2012, Ridgewood, NJ, where we lived, and Manhattan, where Vanessa lived, among many other places, were hit by a powerful hurricane named Sandy. Sandy caused more than seventy billion dollars in damage and two hundred eighty-five deaths.

As Sandy advanced north, we started to feel its effects and follow, on the news, the devastation it was leaving behind. Ridgewood was hit very hard. The intensity of the wind brought down trees, and power lines were destroyed and left lying in the streets. Some neighborhoods were being looted as alarms and video monitoring were down without any Internet or electricity. At our house, we also didn't have electricity, heat, or the use of any of our appliances, so Roberta, Coco, and I were coping as best as possible. There were many traffic issues, and because of the flooding in lower Manhattan, much of the city was at a complete standstill.

As the first day passed, the coldness of the house got into my bones, and that situation reminded me of many years before, when I was a student in La Plata, the cold, damp days of waking up at 4 A.M. to study, wrapped in blankets. After the second day, much to Vanessa's urging and despite Roberta being nervous about leaving our home unalarmed and unprotected, we decided to drive into Manhattan and stay with Vanessa. Although much of New York was affected, it was mostly lower and midtown Manhattan. Vanessa was luckily living just a few blocks north of the cut-off line between those having and not having electricity.

Vanessa was unable to get into work for over a week because everything in Soho, the neighborhood where she worked at the time had no electricity or way to operate, and many of the places had some flooding or water issues. We wound up having several days together, and it was a lovely and quiet family time. Coco was very happy to be among all of us all day and night. She enjoyed walking the streets of Manhattan with all its noises. In the afternoons, we would often walk the streets together, sometimes stopping for a bite to eat, mostly at a local Italian restaurant where I could speak Italian to the waiters. They were pleased to bring us some tasty dishes not well known to the average New Yorker and with a refined Italian appetite like mine!

Oddly enough, storm Sandy and its days of inconveniences and bad weather brought me closer to Vanessa, who grew up hardly ever seeing me, except for my back and forth to the hospital or to notice my beeper going off and my leaving again. We had a chance to chat and leisurely stroll around, and for me to finally see what some of her daily life was like. After a few days, we returned to our home in Ridgewood, and once again, I went back to my daily routine. On the outside, it seemed nothing had happened, and those days in New York were just a memory. For me, however, they were much more because those days of nearness to Vanessa made me aware of how much I missed in all her years growing up. This is life. Unfortunately, a hunter can't chase after two rabbits that run in opposite directions.

I have learned that sometimes, when we are faced with an inconvenience that alters our life, it's easy to get frustrated and unhappy because our daily routine is disturbed. If you allow it, when the chaos ends, sometimes something positive or fortuitous is brought into our lives — Che la vita.

VANESSA'S WEDDING: Vanessa was married on May 10th, 2014. She was married in Watermill, NY, out in the Hamptons. It was a lovely, easy-going, intimate ceremony. We all went out to a lovely dinner, and it was a beautiful day. A week later, on May 17th, 2014, Roberta and I threw the newlyweds a party for all of our family and friends at the Mandarin Oriental Hotel in New York City. Roberta and I spent that weekend at this lovely hotel, and I was anxious the morning of the party. It was a beautiful morning, and I decided to take a long walk in Central Park around the lake. I took many pictures, and while I was admiring the nature of the park, I felt at peace knowing my daughter had found a companion of her heart and was embarking on a new phase of her life. I prayed for a wonderful marriage for Vanessa and for her to be happy and healthy. All the time, there is the nostalgic thought that your baby is gone, and knowing the tragedy of my life and its experiences, I still worry about Vanessa and whatever the future holds for her. As her father, I will pray for her forever because I love her and want the best for her.

The party turned out to be a wonderful affair. Vanessa didn't select a traditional wedding dress but rather a white evening gown, and she looked very elegant. We had a lovely, lively band and people danced all night. Even some of our old Teaneck friends and new Florida friends (more on that later) came in for the affair. Because Vanessa wanted more of a fun, fancy party than the traditional reception, instead of a wedding cake, she surprised my wife with a birthday cake, the top of which was a picture of Coco.

The following Monday, Vanessa left on her honeymoon and returned about two weeks later. Our beautiful granddaughter, Lennon, was born just shy of a year later, and we couldn't have been more thrilled to receive such a gift.

CHRISTMAS TIME IN NEW YORK (December 2017): Roberta, Vanessa, and I decided to take Lennon into the city for a day. Like her mother, Lennon has always been taken in by the sights and sounds of the city, even as an infant. And because she often goes there with Vanessa, she has developed her own admiration for this vast city. I have always been one to relish in the sanctity and quiet of my own home, but I have found sometimes I will make an exception to this for my Lennon.

We took the NJ ferry into midtown and walked over to Rockefeller Plaza to see the holiday decorations, lights, and so many tourists coming into this vibrant city that seems to be the envy of the world. We admired the skyscrapers and saw the expansion of the Javitz Center. The weather was very cold, and in order to enjoy the city at this time of the year, it is imperative to dress in layers. Along with the wind, watery eyes, and stiff face, the cold feels as if it reaches into your bones. Between the cold and walking, after a few hours, we stopped at Il Gattopardo, a nice Italian restaurant. The meal was well enjoyed, and after lunch, we continued our exploration of the city.

Lennon was well bundled up for this occasion in her stroller and its sleeping bag, taking in all the sights and movements. It's amazing to see all the technology and apparatus they have for babies and young children these days. As we were walking, every so often, Lennon would rotate her head to look back and make sure Roberta, her Nonna (grandmother in Italian), was pushing her stroller. To Lennon, Nonna is the official pusher, and heaven help anyone else who tries. When she saw Vanessa had taken over at one point, she would highly protest by loudly exclaiming her preference. Nonna has a very special place in Lennon's heart.

Just in time for our legs to be fatigued, we reached our destination, Radio City Music Hall, to see the Christmas Show and the Rockettes. For anyone unfamiliar with this, it is an annual Christmas Spectacular known to the City of New York. Everything was very beautiful: the music, special effects, and performers. Lennon, being so young, tolerated most of the show until it reached a moment when she became tired of sitting and wished to move about. Out of respect for other patrons, Vanessa took Lennon into the lobby to view the remainder of the show from there while running around. Sure enough, Lennon made some friends with other young children who were brought out during the show too. The number of people who attend this show is amazing, and to exit it is quite something and very challenging.

We once again forged outside into the cold and decided to stop for a quick warm coffee. While in Starbucks, Vanessa realized there was no restroom, so we ran across the street and stopped in a hotel lobby, where Vanessa could tend to Lennon. New York City is amazing in this regard. It was a beautiful day spent with my family, taking in the sights of the holiday season and seeing and feeling the energy of its people, and knowing this city is the capital of the world. Who would have ever imagined I would be in the center of the world, enjoying this time with my family in New York City?

# Chapter 22
# Welcome Argentinians

ABOUT MY BROTHER: As I previously mentioned, my brother, Antonio, and I have eight years between us. From an early age, whenever he was around people, he was the center of attention. He has always had a pleasant personality and has been jovial. When I left for the Jovenado, my brother was only three years old. As such, we really never grew up together. He grew up to be an outdoor person who likes fishing and hunting. He pursued work as a plumber but never wanted to study; this was a major source of frustration for my father. As much as my father was similar to my brother in their activities, my brother's focus on good times annoyed my father.

While at National (public high school), sometimes my friends and I and some girls from our class would gather in the square in Azul to talk and laugh. One day, Antonio came along with me. Right away, he was joking, and it was like he had known everyone forever. He was immediately accepted and began chatting with this one girl in particular, Letti, who was a few years older than him. They began dating, and years later, they were married.

Antonio and Letti have two daughters, both older than Vanessa; one is now an architect, and the other is a lawyer. My brother and I haven't often seen eye to eye on life, and I don't know if it stems from our age difference, that I grew up as a young child during the war in Italy, or whether it's because I was sent away to school, whether it's because I have always been the serious one and he the social one or whether its because we live thousands of miles away from each other and have for decades. For any or all of those reasons, we have never had a close relationship, and it's not uncommon for us to go for long periods without connecting.

During one of these times, I reached out to my brother and invited his daughters here for the summer. I had never met them; they were about fifteen and thirteen, and Vanessa was about eleven. They met Vanessa, and we showed them all around. Roberta took the girls to places like Six Flags Great Adventure, and I took them all over New York City and the mall, etc. They had never been to this country and were in awe of everything. I felt proud I was able to show and expose them to so many things.

The visit went well, so my brother and I began communicating more. One year, for my father's eightieth birthday, my father and I bought tickets for my brother, his wife, and two daughters to fly to Italy for the Christmas holiday. I left a few days ahead of Vanessa and Roberta so I could see my brother and his family and take them around Italy by car. We had not been together as a family since my brother's wedding several decades before.

The night before Roberta and Vanessa were scheduled to fly, as luck would have it, Vanessa wound up in the emergency room with a bad case of tonsillitis. Unfortunately, this was not the first time she had suffered from this, and she was given antibiotics and pain medicine. They missed their flight, and Roberta had to rebook tickets for the following day.

Coincidentally, a few months before I flew to Italy, a patient came to see me in my office. He was an Italian gentleman who worked for the airline, Alitalia. He was suffering from recurring episodes of infection of the gallbladder and was scared to death. I recommended laparoscopic surgery. The surgery went fine; he did very well and went home the same day. After a few hours, he called his mother in Italy from the hospital, and she couldn't believe he was walking and could go home that day. He was very appreciative of what I did and, unbeknownst to me when I was in the airport, someone from Alitalia came and brought me into first class. In gratitude, this dear man had upgraded my flight. For me, this was incredibly special, and he did the same for my wife and daughter.

Although Vanessa spent the first two days of the trip in bed, we all had a lovely time. Many people came over to celebrate with my family and see my brother and me after all the years. After the first five days or so, Vanessa and Roberta flew to Paris for a quick peek at the city, and I took my brother and his family down through the south of Italy all the way to Sicily. We had a lovely time seeing the historical places.

One year, when Vanessa was about eighteen, I suggested to Roberta that we should invite and fly in my nieces for Christmas. Roberta agreed, and so we made arrangements for them to fly. Roberta decided to surprise me and fly in my brother and his wife. Looking back, I should have picked up on all the times she was shushing me out of the room while she was on the phone or telling me to run outside for something, but I never noticed, being so busy and preoccupied with work. It turned out she was ordering extra mattresses and finding an extension for our dinner table so we could all eat together. Security at airports was very different then, and we were allowed to obtain passes to go to the gate and wait for my nieces to disembark from the plane. As we were waiting, at one point, I saw my nieces, and as I was embracing them, I felt a tap on my shoulder, and I heard, *"Hola, hermano."* I turned around to see my brother smiling and Letti alongside him. I couldn't believe it! I later learned that Roberta had one of our friend's receptionists who spoke Spanish contact my brother, and she helped coordinate and make all their travel arrangements.

We took them shopping and to Atlantic City and spent the holiday together with our family in Connecticut and some of Roberta's family from Philadelphia and South Jersey. It was during the visit to Connecticut my Aunt Giuseppina pulled me aside and stated she thought my brother was perhaps somewhat a little envious of my success. To me, this was incredulous given how much more pleasant his first thirty years were compared to mine, but looking back, I think she saw what I was blind to. I was so proud to share my life and show my brother and his family my world.

While my brother and his family were here, we completed applications for them to come permanently to this country. I told them I would help them get started, as I knew it would be difficult. It took about six or seven years for them to be approved, and then, suddenly, they decided not to come. We again slowly lost touch.

Eventually, with time, my older niece, the architect, married a doctor, also a surgeon, in Argentina. One year, only a few years ago, they came to Miami, and she said she wished to speak with and see me. I drove to where they were staying, and I met her husband. We had so much in common, and since then, they have been coming to visit Roberta and me every year. We keep in contact throughout the year via video calls. It's such incredible technology!

Vanessa comes down to Florida to share in these visits, and Lennon now comes along too. The evening of everyone's arrival on the first of these trips was very pleasant and special. Sergio was meeting Roberta, Vanessa, and Lennon for the first time. We spent many beautiful days together, and those days and hours flew by very quickly. We were all so delighted to be together one more time.

To them, this visit was something very different. Although neither Roberta nor Vanessa speaks Spanish, they can communicate in their own unique way. With a little bit of broken Italian and lots of hand and facial expressions, we all understood each other. When everyone was confused and unable to get their respective points across, I would step in as the official translator. One amazing thing stands out in my mind. Lennon was only two-and-a-half at this time. One afternoon, after lunch, Sergio and Eugenia retired to their bedroom to relax. After a short time, Lennon followed. Quickly, you could hear all of them laughing and talking as if there was no language barrier at all. Lennon was front and center and had engaged my niece and her husband into her world; she mesmerized them, and she knew it. This alone was a wonderful moment for them and me as well.

We spoke a lot about the past and family problems and where those things are today. Eugenia and I are similar and see many things in the same light. The weather was lovely, so we went biking along the long and winding golf cart pathways from our home in The Villages to one of the town centers. We admired the meticulously maintained flowers and greenery while we rode under huge Spanish moss trees . At night, in the town squares, there is live music. People dance, have a drink, and socialize. The squares are all surrounded by restaurants, shops, and a movie theater. I had tremendous joy watching Lennon dance and run with other children, all of them trying to keep rhythm with the music. You could see her joy and happiness. That picture will remain in my mind forever. At home, we cooked. Although we did not do the asado criollo (way of grilling), we did barbecue American style, and our guests enjoyed trying everything.

My niece loves to shop and they visited many areas and stores. She purchased various things for herself, Sergio, and their children. She informed us that many of the items purchased in the United States are better quality and less expensive for her than in Argentina, so she filled up suitcase after suitcase, and her great worry was that they would be overweight and they would have to pay extra. Luckily this did not occur; Roberta and I had an extra bag or two to help keep each bag to the right weight.

It was a very emotional farewell. Every time it's time to say goodbye, I think of when I would visit my parents in Italy, and when the time to leave came, there were many hugs and tears. For my mother, her tears were always so great they would interrupt her words. She used to say, "Figlio chi sa cuando ci rivedremo?" (Who knows when we will be able to see each other?) I would embrace her and tell her I would be back again soon. As the years passed, it was more difficult for me to convince her I would return while she was still alive, and she, with resignation, would bend her head and say, "*Chi sa*" (who knows). I used to tell her, "Mama, do not think such bad things, and she, in a whisper, used to mumble, "*Ci sono I anni*" (I am old).

My father, who seemed to be the strongest, would intervene, separating us and comforting her with the words, "Antoinette, he will return soon." Those separations are very sad. In nature, even mother animals show their torment and unease if their babies are separated from them. The dream is for a child to be close to their mother for her warmth and protection. That is the way I felt when we said goodbye. Because I have experienced so many years of separation from my family, and I see the years going by, those memories are still as fresh in my mind as if they were today. Thank you for coming. It was a great pleasure seeing you again. I hope you enjoyed your time here. If this is so, the separation will not be bitter but filled with memories of happiness together as a family.

Roberta and I had plans to meet Eugenia and Sergio in Disney this summer, and I was going to be fortunate enough to meet Eugenia and Sergio's two children on this visit. Lennon and Vanessa were also planning to fly down for a few days. It was going to be a lovely family affair. Sadly, the Coronavirus has altered our plans. More on this later.

# Chapter 23: Reflections

Our lives are composed of many moments and memories, both beautiful and things that have caused us pain. As the years continue, many memories and thoughts pass through my mind. Memories have come to mean and represent different things to me as I have continued to gain experiences and, fortunately, wisdom. Thinking back to the hard days of my youth, I realize the limitations my parents had. My parents lost everything. They had to leave their land, country, family, friends, customs, and language. They made these selfless sacrifices in the hope of a better future for my brother and me. They spoke broken Spanish and were young and isolated in a foreign land. Despite my parents' constant struggle, they always told me to work hard, reach for the top and never give up. My life has changed a lot from those days, and the adversities I witnessed became my driving force of strength and determination to succeed and get ahead in this world. Whatever success I have achieved is my eternal thank you for their continued sacrifice.

One morning, when I was a student at the University, I was reading the morning newspaper and learned that the opera, *Barber of Seville,* would be played on the radio that afternoon. My roommate was kind enough to let me borrow his radio because I didn't have one of my own. It was a weekend, and as I mentioned, most of my contemporaries were away on the weekends having fun in Buenos Aires. I was so pleased to have the room all to myself. I closed the shutters and door to block the noise coming from the street. The silence offered me the chance to truly appreciate the music I loved so much and to lose myself in the beauty of the story. I held the radio close to my ear and leaned into the radio to hear every sound of the music. In those few hours,

I enjoyed being alone in the darkness. It gave me the solitude needed to transport myself into a different world. This genre of music has and still does give me so much pleasure.

Almost fifty years have passed since then. Fifty years seems to be a long time, but in reality, it's flown by. Many things happened during those years; there were a lot of ups and downs. The memories have become more acute and surface more frequently, although I do not know why. Perhaps on my way up the mountain and now having reached its peak, I can look down at the valley below and see and remember the arduous route taken. What gives me more pleasure is that despite all the adversities I encountered, I never lost hope of seeing a better day. The occasional nightmares that surface in my dreams seem to last an eternity and seem so real. However, upon awakening, I realize this is precisely what they were, a dream from the past. Little by little, my pulse slows, and calmness is reestablished. This calmness is best exemplified when I enjoy my music. My mind is free, and whatever tension I have leaves me.

Sometimes the free feeling from the music reminds me of my father-in-law. We shared a passion for this music, and when he was Dean of the Philadelphia School of Performing Arts, we would often attend different concerts given by his students and professors. One afternoon, we were on the way to one such function. My father-in-law was driving, I was in the passenger seat, and my mother-in-law and Roberta were in the back seat. We were listening to the Beethoven Piano Concerto Number 5, *Call of the Emperor*. The gentle passages of the music and the tender, touching melody were moving; I was lost in the beauty of the music. My father-in-law's voice brought me out of my trance. He mentioned how much he would like to play this piano concerto with his students before retiring. My present solace in the music quickly became a big knot in my stomach, and a deep, internal scream overcame me; I knew his sickness would prevent this dream from ever coming true.

I think of my simple life in Argentina as a boy. During my youth, because of the need for money and the misery that existed after World War II, I became aware of many things at a young age. I saw there were no jobs and no ability to earn money, which clearly affected the quality of life of any family present. At that time, the man of the household struggled to find work outside the home. However, it was the woman of each household that kept the home's internal economy going. It was the women whose natural instincts managed to achieve and produce miracles each day, even when rationing food. I saw all the women in my family saving what they could, thinking about tomorrow, mainly depriving themselves and making many sacrifices. This was the life my mother endured even when she moved to Argentina.

My mother survived because of her ability to multitask, and her knowledge of life's practicalities learned from a young age. At that time, our wardrobe was very limited, and the quality of our clothing was not the best. Because we had so little, we wore things daily, and they quickly showed the signs of a strenuous life as visible holes appeared. My dear mother would spend her precious time mending and repairing the worn-out clothes my father used and needed for his daily work. Sometimes she was able to patch the clothing with similar material, but when no match was available, she did the best she could under the circumstances, and when repaired, her work came to resemble a medieval parade full of many colors. She even would mend the holes in our socks, an art that is lost today, thanks to industrialization. Although this may seem incredible to some, particularly younger generations, this was how we lived. If you just sat and waited, the bus would never come. You had to try very hard to succeed, and even more so if you had big ambitions for your future, it was best you kept your dream to yourself because if you revealed such a dream, you would be the laughing stock of everyone.

Sharing the meals outside with my parents, our gatherings were just an expression of something possible. In reality, to reach those dreams due to our circumstances and the environment was just a deep feeling and desire for something better for our future lives. Those evenings we shared our meals were real, while all the other things were like castles built in the air, and we would look at the sky and fantasize, inventing imaginative figures until the wind blew and changed the landscape. That was my life at the time. I never imagined those dreams one day becoming a reality. It was a long course. Like Dante says in *The Inferno*, "*Perso in quella foresta oscura.*" (Somebody before me got lost, but because of luck, Virgil was there to guide him and show the way.) We may have lived in what some would call misery, but there was love because we defined what a true family was. Remembering those days, I become nostalgic.

More than sixty years ago, during my days in Azul, I had what I understood to be good friends. Economically, my friends were in a better position than I was. Being well-off placed my friends better off socially, too; this remains true today in many places. Both their money and connections brought prestige; it was like having the key to a locked door. This premise was even the same during olden times when the Guelphs and the Ghibellines fought in Florence. Those who possessed a name like Cavalcanti, Donatti, or Medici held a superior status, and power and future matrimonial arrangements were made and promised as fortunes multiplied. Of course, I did not possess a unique name, and on more than one occasion, when I was in someone's house as a teenager when introduced to a friend's parents, I noticed some were very gracious and diplomatic with their salutations toward the sons and daughters of the well-known town residents. The conversations with the notable sons and daughters lasted longer, and they were treated with cordiality and awareness, while my introductions had a different tone. This did not go unnoticed by me. At the time, though, given the circumstances, what could I do? Who was I to tell them that one day I would be someone important too? They would have never believed me anyway.

According to the thinking of that time, I was nothing but a dreamer. One can't forget that when Columbus was in front of the professors at the university in Salamanca (the geniuses of the time), he also was called a dreamer because they disapproved of his theory of reaching the Indies by going west. In the end, though, who are really the ones living in their own dream? I remember my mother once presented an analogy of common sense to me. It was about two women in a beauty contest. If a woman finds a discrepancy in another woman's appearance, she will never point it out to her. To do so would essentially give the win to the other contestant. *"Lavati la faccia così tu sei più bella di me."*(Wash your face so you are prettier than me).

As you know, I had a group of friends from the National school that used to come to join us to eat at my parent's home. Of all these friends today, I am in contact with only one. It seems the memory of my friendship with the others was quickly forgotten once I earned my stripes as an American doctor. Throughout the years, I felt inspired to make contact again, as my curiosity to reconnect was insatiable, but even this small pleasure, up until today, has been denied to me. I remember at my brother's wedding in Argentina, I ran into a former colleague from National at the bar. When I saw my old friend standing alone, I went to say hello. I received a very icy reception as though I were an alien from a different planet. I will never know if he finished his studies at the school we both formerly attended. He was completely disinterested in having a conversation with me.

Many years ago, I tried to reach an old roommate with whom I shared a room for seven years as a student in La Plata. My wife, having grown frustrated with my search, as this was through an International operator before the days of the Internet, used her smarts and was able to locate a different friend, living in one of the provinces of Argentina, who knew my other friend and was able to put us in touch. It was lovely for us to connect finally. We spoke for a long time, and everything was going well until I mentioned my life in the States. I mentioned I was a surgeon here, and when he asked about my parents, I said they were again living in Italy and I saw them each year. I was hoping that my joy of being able to share my current life would be matched, but I noticed a distance all of a sudden. My friend instantly seemed uncomfortable. Before hanging up, I told him I would phone again and perhaps he could write to me in the meantime. He said he didn't have time for that, and I knew this would be our last conversation. Needless to say, the primordial joy vanished the moment we hung up the phone.

On another occasion, I was able to contact a doctor colleague of mine who I had studied with in La Plata. This particular friend went to work in Israel, and because of the Internet, we were able to relive so many memories. He vividly remembered my parents and our dinners in Azul. He was sunny and bright, and I was filled with joy and happiness for him after hearing about his life. I then took my turn, filling him in on where I was now living and, what I was doing, that I had a family. After I shared, despite our conversation being so lovely, I never heard from him again. I tried to reach him again quite a few times, but my attempts went unanswered. I stopped trying.

I decided to write about all this because the topic came up while golfing this morning with my friend, a retired military judge. My friend and I share a mutual respect and admiration for one another, and our friendship became stronger as he learned more about me. Anyway, I was telling him about my experience with these past colleagues in Argentina and my desire to hear from them. He looked at me and said, "Sal, look what you have accomplished in your life. I know what you all went through, but they don't. They see your final outcome and base their feelings on that. Who cares then?" That was his final answer. It's too bad some things have to be this way. I thought my former colleagues would be proud of this once young, poor boy who grew up and lost his timidity after his long journey and was able to finally see the other side of the mountain.

There will always be naysayers, critics, and those you can never please. Take joy in other people's hard work and accomplishments. Share pride and happiness for other humans. It's an important, gracious quality, one that makes your soul kind and very easy to love and respect.

SETBACKS: There are certain times in our lives when everything seems to come to a crashing halt because there is no way out and no hope. As you know, my father had been a manual worker all his life, applying himself with dedication and without complaint. He was always in constant motion. Whenever he started something, he had a tremendous determination to finish whatever he was doing. I don't know exactly why, but a moment came when my father made an appointment with a young cardiologist who had recently opened a practice in Azul. I was either finishing college or in my first year of medical school at this time. Anyway, in a short time, this young cardiologist became very popular. At the time, many of the older doctors were not available or, because of their age, had never specialized in any medical discipline; those gentlemen used to spend more time caring for their cows than their patients. For all these reasons, my father made an appointment with this young doctor and went to his office for an examination.

My father returned home that day a different man. He was diagnosed with an aneurysm of the aorta arch (aneurysm is a distention of the walls of the arteries, and like a balloon that keeps expanding, the moment comes when it will pop. A person with this disease is a time bomb; if the aneurysm is not taken care of, there is a high chance of the person not surviving). My father changed. He was very worried, and all of his singing stopped. Our home was no longer the same place and felt like a funeral parlor. There was no place for open discussion. It was a very dark moment in our lives.

Given that this was more than sixty years ago in a small town, this was like a death sentence for my father. He was forced to retire early and be at home all day. His forced inactivity drove him crazy; he always said he felt like he couldn't breathe sitting so still. My mother was devastated. She was aware of the consequences and was slowly preparing to lose her husband. This disease became a time bomb for both of my parents; it was killing them. They often argued about what he could and could not do. Finally, at some juncture, my father couldn't take it anymore and gradually started doing things around the house. He figured if he was going to die, he might as well die happy and doing what he enjoyed.

We were all very worried for my dad and saddened and scared at the idea of losing him. Besides being our father and blood, practically speaking, he was the only provider for us. My mother would often speak to me in private. I would try to offer her hope and, whenever possible, any advice I had, although I know I was not very convincing. She would turn away, lower her head and walk to a different part of the house to console herself. Sadly, she would cry by herself until she was exhausted.

At the time, we felt like someone was constantly pointing a loaded gun at us. That was a terrible time we went through. As it turned out, all my father's activities didn't affect him. The reason for this is that many years later, we found out the doctor had incorrectly x-rayed my father and misdiagnosed him. My father never had an aneurysm. He lived to be ninety-nine and a half years old. He wound up returning to work. He remained active all his life and bicycled till his early nineties. The irony is that my dad outlived the young cardiologist by many decades.

A few nights ago I decided to watch an Italian movie called *Nuovo Cinema Paradiso*. It's not the first time I have seen this movie, but for some reason, this time was different and very emotional. It seemed as though a few passages of the film were speaking to me. I kept asking myself why the movie impacted me so much, and I concluded that I realized more and more that as life continues, you can never take back a lost moment or opportunity.

*Nuovo Cinema Paradiso* is a story that takes place in a small Italian village many years ago. There was poverty, the people were simple, and there was not too much to do. The main event was when a film was shown in the main square. The people of the village would gather around in their chairs to watch the movie and pass the time. In the film, there was a character named Toto, a young child, who befriended the projectionist and brought food to this gentleman every day. One day, the projector caught fire, and the projectionist was trapped in the showing room and could not escape. Aware of what was happening, Toto came to the rescue and dragged the man down the stairs, saving his life. However, the projectionist lost his vision and could no longer work, so Toto took over the job even though he was a child.

The projectionist was a paternal companion to Toto. Over the years, he encouraged Toto to pursue a career in Rome, saying there was more to life outside their small village. Toto followed his advice, eventually becoming a senior executive. Years later, Toto returned to his home village to attend the funeral of this dear old friend who had passed away. There is an emotional scene between Toto and his mother, who is now much older, and she kindly reveals to her son her wish to see him marry. (*Il vederlo sistemato.*) She wished for this so her soul could be tranquil and one day rest in peace.

This scene brought back memories of the conversations I used to have with my mother during my visits to Italy. Although I was a grown man, to my mother, I was still her baby boy. Because of the distance between us, during the months between our visits, she would constantly think of my family and pray for us. Upon my arrival, as soon as we were alone, she would glance at me, revealing that she wanted to tell me so many things but was hesitant to do so. I could sense her timidity in wanting to share her thoughts. I would begin chatting to put her at ease, then, all of a sudden, with much love and joy, she would share everything she had been keeping in. It was like a waterfall of information.

There are moments in our lives one remembers, although the days are gone. I know those days will not come back, but their memory will exist as long as I live. Yet there are times when I wonder if there was anything I could have done or said to my mother to have made our special time even better? Was there something I missed? Sometimes I feel a heaviness and sadness in my heart because perhaps I did not embrace her against my chest and kiss her enough when she sat just across from me. Sometimes I feel guilty thinking about those days because she is no longer here, and I question if she knew how much I deeply loved and cared for her. I miss you, Mom.

These thoughts bring me back to the film. As I mentioned, Toto was a young boy who grew up in a small village. As a teenager, he fell in love with a girl, Elena, from the same village. However, her parents disapproved of him because they felt he would not accomplish anything and decided to send Elena away. Before Elena left, she and Toto arranged to meet in the square to say their goodbyes. Toto waited, but Elena never came. Forlorn, Toto followed his mentor's advice and went to live and work in Rome.

While Toto was away in Rome, his friend, the projectionist, passed away. When Toto returned for his friend's funeral, he saw a beautiful young girl who reminded him of his former love. Toto inquired where Elena lived and called her from the public telephone across the street. He learned she was married to one of his former friends, and they had a daughter. He asked to see her, but she declined since so many years had passed, and circumstances had changed. Toto went to the beach to sit on the rocks where they used to spend many moments, and while he was there, despairing, he saw a car approaching, and Elena came to him. Toto asked about her absence the day of their goodbye years before, and Elena explained she had come but was late because the bus was running behind schedule. They embrace, realizing they both truly loved one another after all. When they were young, they loved each other and made promises never realized because of her parents' objections, circumstances, and misunderstandings. All of this was like a wall blocking the culmination of their dreams. The fire of youth was reduced to ashes, but under those ashes, there remained a kindling fire that just needed a little bit of wind to give life to those flames of forgotten love.

When I was young, I read a phrase that has stuck with me to this day: all things that happened in the past were better than today. Youth is the spring of our lives. Everything is green, the flowers are blossoming, and insects carry pollen to make nectar for new plants. This creates new life. All this seems to follow a logical rhythm that symbiosis and fraternity are examples of what life should be. Nature reminds us every year that the spring season is fleeting, and insects and animals work very hard to build a reserve for the inclement weather that will follow. All that is common sense, and I admire this. During our youth, we are full of energy, run from one place to another, and everything is beautiful. Our passion finds solace, and we share happiness with friends. That pleasant atmosphere makes us ambitious to plan for the future. On many occasions, a fantasy embellishes our dream, but there are other times when that fantasy can work against us.

On more than one occasion, when I was in the operating room, I would listen to other personnel's conversations when they would speak about their dreams and upcoming weddings: preparations, flowers, limos, etc. Everything seemed to be so beautiful and well planned. At home, having dinner with my wife, I wouldn't share this information, and I used to feel uncomfortable because I knew some of these colleagues were planning things beyond their means. I used to tell my wife everything sounded beautiful, but I would hear in those conversations future plans of how the newlyweds were going to succeed in life, individually and together.

One has to sacrifice now, in the present, so you can one day harvest what you sow. This is what my wife and I did. We discussed this before we were married because it was of paramount importance to me, and I needed to make sure Roberta was on board. Our life followed a path of discipline because we knew our spring would not last forever and that eventually, the winter would arrive. I remember sadly that on more than one occasion, several months after a colleague's wedding day, they seemed to be unhappy. Not knowing what had happened, I would approach someone I was friendlier with to inquire if this person was alright. I would often be told one spouse had left for another person or the relationship wasn't working out, and now there were so many expenses. All those happy dreams lasted only a few years and, sometimes, months.

It's imperative to communicate and plan in life. If you do, your winter will be manageable, tolerable, and perhaps even pleasant. That being said, it's exceedingly important to study and look to history as a guide, as history does repeat itself.

# Chapter 24
# History Repeats Itself

Looking back at history, the Roman Empire was initially comprised of dedicated citizens who sacrificed for common goals. As they became wealthier, some became lazy and corrupt; we all know what this led to and its final outcome. It's been said that history repeats itself, and I believe this to be true. I guess it parallels the cycle of our lives; things have to get worse before they get better. It is the irony of our lives; for me, it's hard to understand because in doing so and gambling with an uncertain destiny, one never knows if those easy times we are enjoying will come back. Are we enjoying ourselves at that moment solely because someone before us prepared the ground with a lot of sacrifice and misery, and now we are simply just harvesting the fruits of their labor? How can we be unappreciative and indifferent to such a reality? To me, the only logical explanation is a profound ignorance of the past and a lack of motivation; this is dangerous. This indifference is like a cancer that will metastasize with time. Who is to blame?

In my memories are the days when I was my father's audience. Sometimes he used to tell me things that perhaps he had kept inside for a long time, like a farmer waiting for the right time to seed his field. My father, like this farmer who had enough seed for only one crop, knowing his family and their lives depended on a fruitful harvest, waited for the right time to open the windows and give freedom to his thoughts. When my father was young, the Italian regime's fascists were in power — because of this, one had to be careful to keep one's personal opinions to oneself. Because history repeats itself, one never can be sure that today's confidant will not be tomorrow's detractor. I guess my father found me to be the right audience at the right time to vent his thoughts. He clearly thought the seed was ready to be planted so I could learn something.

As you know, my parents were poor and had limited income. When they were growing up, during the fascist regime, no matter what you believed, you were considered a member of the governing party and had to follow the rules they dictated. In this regard, it was demanded of my father by the local community powers that he buy two fascist uniforms. This did not sit well with my father, and one day he presented himself at the fascist center, which was full of people, and told one of the bosses his family couldn't afford to buy two uniforms. He said he could buy one and appreciate the other to be free, as a distant relative had made and received such an arrangement. My father quickly learned this was a mistake because he was grabbed by his neck and buttocks in front of everyone present and thrown into the middle of the street. When he tried to stand, he was kicked back down and was obviously very humiliated. Again, being a small town, it was just a matter of time before everyone would learn of this incident.

As the years passed, the regime failed because of the injustices many suffered from those in power. In fact, many of the formerly oppressed who were angry and now free came to claim their retribution. History tells of the atrocities committed and how some people were afraid to walk on the street because of possible repercussions. This was so much so that one day, the distant relative mentioned above, who happened to be the mother of the chief fascist who, years before, beat up and humiliated my father, came to visit my grandmother. Knowing the wrongs committed, particularly to my father that day, in a somewhat distrustful way, she threw herself onto her knees before my grandmother and, with a dispirited cry, begged my grandmother for forgiveness and pleaded with her not to report her son to the new authorities.

Those were sad days. History repeatedly shows those at the top and in power think their power will last forever. They don't realize that, like life, all is fleeting, and like a rotating wheel that is at the top one moment, it will find itself down the next. Like in Mozart's opera, *Don Giovanni*, at the end, after the protagonist goes into the fires of hell, the assistant says, "*Questo e' il fin di chi fa mal.*" (This is the end of he who does bad things.) What I find equally dangerous in today's world is when I watch television, usually a newscast, and see students on various college campuses or the streets of a city share their opinion in response to a reporter's question or some recent societal ongoings. Sadly, and more dangerously, important, I find more often than not that such young persons don't even have minimal knowledge about something they should be fluent about. This makes me feel like crying because I think of all those around the world who are unable to pursue a dream or even get a basic education because of the local lack of resources. How many brains and lives are wasted when so many motivated young people would grab it if given an opportunity? Then we have many in this country, with all its resources and opportunities, waiting for handouts. Sadly, this "epidemic" has existed for quite some time in this country. I remember, years ago, being present for the dedication of one of my friend's new buildings. A senator from Washington, who was a friend of my friend, came to make a speech. Afterward, I recall this senator telling my friend he had just returned from Silicon Valley, where the local authorities informed him of the need for thousands of engineers, preferably from India, because they had proved reliable and appreciated their jobs.

There is no status quo in our lives. On May 8, 1794, civilization lost a great human being, Antoine Lavoisier, at fifty years old. The guillotine executed Antoine. That day the world lost a creative soul who, because of his genius, was at the mercy of fanatics and the mobs running the country at the time. This was a common consequence of the abuses and exploitation through the centuries until the moment the starving and oppressed said, enough is enough, and proceeded, like a hurricane, that, without any distinction, destroyed everything and everyone in its path. However, the desire for revenge and its actual damage does not improve anyone's situation because those at the bottom are more fragile and unprepared to confront yet another adverse problem. They are always the ones who suffer the most; thus, history seems to repeat itself.

In 429 B.C., the great legislator, Pericles, died in Athens during the plague. The Peloponnesian War brought misery and starvation, and people literally dropped dead in the middle of the streets every day. Death was so rampant that there came a time when nobody cared to collect the cadavers for burial, and there was no hope on the horizon. In facing this adversity, many found temporary pleasure as a sweet release to the predictable end of death, and thus came the expression, "Let's be happy today because tomorrow we are going to die." This was how many faced their sad destiny.

Throughout various centuries the world has faced many similar calamities and devastation in which millions of victims, not knowing why, faced such horrible destinies. It was unknown why such things happened, and because of this, there was a bitter resignation to share a common collective misery; or as an Argentinian saying dictates, "Mal de muchos consuelo de tontos." (The collective suffering gives consolation to fools.) For example, in 541, the Justinian plague devastated the Byzantine Empire, claiming up to ten thousand victims in a day. In 1347, during the One Hundred Years War, the Black Death claimed between seventy-five to two hundred million lives in Europe. During this time, Boccaccio wrote his masterpiece, *The Decameron*. This famous, historical piece tells of the history of seven men and seven women in Florence who escaped the city and isolated themselves in a successful attempt to survive. These fourteen individuals were in direct contrast to the Athenians during the plague that killed Pericles, who were busy partying, drinking, and attending social gatherings, which only led to their demise. Without realizing it, these fourteen individuals, centuries ago, were practicing the isolation we are doing today during the Covid-19 epidemic.

When Christopher Columbus came to America, so did many European diseases, like smallpox, typhus, and malaria, previously unknown to America and to which the local population had no immunity. Sadly, the American communities of the time suffered the consequences. It is estimated that over the course of one hundred and fifty years, more than ninety-five percent of the Native American population at that time perished, nearly exterminating the race. The Spanish flu pandemic of 1918-1920 was very contagious, claiming more than fifty million victims and infecting over five hundred million people. Today, in 2020, we are faced with the global pandemic of Covid-19, also called the Coronavirus. This virus seems to have originated in Wuhan, China, and in a very brief time, spread all over the world. Because of today's technology and transportation, and because of the interconnection of national economies, in one way or another, we are all at risk of infection and its consequences.

As we discussed, humanity has faced similar conditions throughout history. Today, however, with more knowledge, observation, and the lightning speed of exchange of ideas and research, some of the diseases of the past that caused so many problems and death have been exterminated or their symptoms alleviated with the introductions of vaccines, the discovery of antibiotics and the knowledge of preventative measures. With the onset of this new Covid-19, we still have a long way to go. During antiquity, when facing a disaster, a scapegoat was needed to justify and explain this 'will of God' because all was based on our sins. In such times, ignorance and fear of the unknown led to a mix of confusion and disorganized thoughts. Sadly, this created a population with a sense of resignation and a lack of hope. Many lowered their heads and retreated to a corner, waiting for the reality to occur.

I can't imagine a mother having her young child taken away from her and not having the ability to prevent this, as Parcae (in Latin mythology, there was a belief this is how one's soul was delivered to its final resting place) was approaching and claiming its victims. It had to be a terrible scene, for it has been represented in such a diabolic form; a skeleton wrapped in a black sheet showing only its face and carrying a sickle. What sad times to invent such terrible myths. My question remains, who will ever find pleasure in such a depiction? I think perhaps such myths were created to keep the population submissive and obedient; this was the justification. I imagine the summation and lack of knowledge further intensified the prevalence of the dark colors of their lives, with their ragged clothing showing skeletal bodies with prominent ribs, signs of continuous starvation, and lack of what is essential to any animal or human.

What I can't comprehend is why in the middle of such adversities, no one listened to those trying to discuss it and left things to the side of misconception. It seems to me, after so many years of greediness, ambitions, and ignorance, the desire for power has not left us, and because of this attitude, perhaps we deserve such calamity, as the seasons bring the yearly changes and renovations, perhaps these adversities in our lives bring changes that reinforce our immunity. Who knows, there is still a lot of pathology unknown about the human body, and the right medicine to cure certain things, like Covid-19, has not been found yet (although there are some promising clinical trials). It is my firm belief we will never completely eradicate these cyclical events. I modestly think finding and distributing a cure worldwide will create different problems as some humans and those in power will forever think themselves to be godly, and it will take a very long time for certain countries or subsets of such countries' populations to receive what others in wealthier, more powerful nations receive quickly. As a society and as individuals, we always need to be wary of such persons because, in the worst situation possible, one deranged and powerful person could one day possibly put an end to the world as we know it. Although it is unlikely, it's always best to be alert and cautious. I don't think such prudence can hurt; after all, what do we have to lose?

MY FRIEND SAL: April 16, 2020, was a sad day for Roberta, Vanessa, and me. Our longtime friend, Sal, sadly succumbed to the Coronavirus. Sal and I first met on William's Island when Roberta and I lived in our condo in the Bella Mare. Sal and his wife, Marie, also purchased a unit, one unit over and one floor up from us. They were so close I could reach their front door in under a minute using one set of the building's service stairs. From the first day we met, Sal and I knew we had some things in common, obviously starting with the fact that we shared the same first name. We both struggled in the early part of life as young men, and we shared the common path of wanting to accomplish something in life and have a better, more stable future.

As our friendship intensified, the secret door that was keeping our past, sad days hidden, opened, and in trusting one another, we were like brothers and shared our stories. He was aware of my difficult upbringing, and I was aware of his. Sal's life was not easy. He had issues with his father, and their relationship was tense. Even at eighty-seven years old, Sal resented these issues and younger days. Sal struggled in school, primarily because of disciplinary reasons. Since the age of eight or nine, he took it upon himself to sell newspapers on the streets and trains at all hours. Because he was so young, he was apprehended by the police on quite a few occasions and brought home to his parents. However, this did not intimidate him, and the next day he was back doing the same thing. Sal earned more money selling newspapers than his father did at his job. He shared his earnings with his mother to support the family and save for the future.

Although at some point Sal was expelled from school, he later earned his high school diploma and went on to run a very successful international shipping company. Despite Sal's poor education, he became a very successful man. He told me the beginnings were very difficult, and he had to deal with unscrupulous people and thieves. I recall he used to tell me all kinds of stories about various things, and being brought up in a different culture and unexposed to such things, I was still somewhat naive, and I would ask how he managed to deal with them; such as having at times to deal with the Mafia. I would ask if he was ever nervous about his family being hurt. He would say no and explain how he was always streetwise and could talk for hours without revealing anything and never compromise. He said he always spoke clearly and followed through; thus, he gained their respect.

Almost weekly, Sal and his wife and Roberta and I would go out to eat together, or sometimes just Sal and I went to a local Spanish restaurant where we would sit and chat and exchange ideas. We used to get together with our wives for a cup of tea. Roberta, knowing Sal enjoyed a good Italian meal, would make a nice pasta sauce, and we would spend a leisurely evening in our apartment together with our friends. I would mention at this juncture that my friend Sal was the one who made me aware of the TV program *Greed* I mentioned in an earlier chapter. I wish I had met him before I made that bad decision!

As I explained before, despite all the precautions and steps taken, my health was getting worse on a daily basis at the Bella Mare. When I told Sal of our decision to leave Bella Mare, he was greatly saddened by this news. He was frustrated and thought us moving to The Villages would disrupt our friendship. We kept in touch via phone and email, and soon after we moved, Marie and Sal came to visit and stay with us for a few days at our new home one hour north of Orlando. Marie and Sal were pleased with what they saw, and not too long after that, they decided to purchase a piece of land of their own; and with Roberta's help, they designed their dream home. Roberta was very involved with the selection of their home's finishes, such as flooring, kitchen cabinets, and appliances, etc. The house is exquisite, and once completed, it took some time to move in. However, once they were settled, they were very happy.

We were geographically close again, with our respective homes less than one mile apart. We had many great days sharing our coffee and meals again, whether at one of our homes or a local establishment. Sadly, the last few months were difficult for all of us. Sal's health began to decline, starting with the curvature of his spine from severe scoliosis that no longer allowed him to walk normally. He also had diabetes, although he had kept this in check for many years.

Then, a few months ago, Sal had a bad fall. Marie phoned, and we went over there. Although we were able to get Sal up, we took him to the hospital to be examined. He was diagnosed with severe stenosis of the aortic valve. This means that when he got excited, his heart was unable to pump enough blood to the brain; probably the precise reason why he fell. After an extensive workup, the decision was made to have a cardiac catheterization to check the condition of his heart. It was discovered that he had severe coronary disease, and at least four stents were needed to provide proper blood flow to his heart. Because his three children are in New York and he was not a good candidate for open-heart surgery, he opted to fly back to NY and have these procedures done there so his children could be around for him and Marie.

During the procedure, they performed a valve replacement through catheterization, and one stent was placed in the coronary artery. However, the other stents could not be put in. We were in touch by telephone, and he was optimistic and looking forward to returning to Florida. I told him not to rush until he was stable, and we would be waiting for him. I was concerned about his coronary disease and diabetes, though. I knew he was still trying to make some major decisions, as he still worked every day, so I tried my best to make him aware of his limitations, as did his wife. Eventually, he was discharged, and we kept in touch from home. He was in good spirits, but then he fell again. He was brought to the hospital and was sadly found to be positive for the coronavirus.

The first day when I spoke to Roberta, he seemed to be doing well and asked for soup. Sadly though, the next day, his oxygen saturation lowered, and he was intubated, put on a respirator, and moved to the ICU. Just a few days later, my dear friend left this earth and passed away. The entire family feels a tremendous emptiness. The idea of not seeing him again or not being able to share those beautiful evenings anymore saddens my soul. I have just my memories left of those days.

During this pandemic, bad news seems to resound daily. Seeing people wearing masks outside the operating room or hospital is a new one, even for me. It seems odd to keep our social distance. Every time I encounter another person walking, I respectfully cross to the other side of the road instead of maybe stopping and exchanging a few words. We all hope and pray for life to return to normal and move on from this virus. I pray a vaccine can be found and manufactured, putting an end to this invisible enemy who took our beloved friend and many, many others.

I will miss the afternoon telephone call from Sal, with his jovial voice, who would invite me to join them for a cup of coffee. He would always tell me Marie was brewing a fresh pot of coffee and tell me to come over. Unfortunately, this is our destiny, and because *Parcae* (carrier of one's soul) never sleeps, the fact is that my friend Sal is no longer with us, and we will miss those days when we were knowledgeable of the present situation. In my head, Mozart's Cosi Fan Tutti reverberates when it's said, *"Ho come in un momento si cangio la sorte mia."* (How in a very short time my life has changed.) I can then say and feel how fleeting life is, and despite all of its beauty, there is the cruel reality of finality. Rest in peace, my friend, Sal. We love you and are forever going to miss you.

# Chapter 25
# A Bit Of Philosophy

We are all born unique. There is always something that differentiates one person from the next. We each have different qualities, think in different ways, and go through our daily lives doing things not equal to or the same as the next person. We follow different life paths. All of these things make each individual very special. Why? Because our brains see and interpret things differently and use this to reason, this is supposed to provide clarity in our life. The glass full versus glass empty scenario best references this. There are those who see the glass as half full and those who see it as half empty. Common sense is a trait that is supposed to give us the ability to interpret what is logical or not. Being logical allows people to communicate their differences while obtaining a better understanding of one another. It is the ability to accept that we don't all think alike; therefore, we should be more tolerant of one another. Common sense is the ability to make judgment calls between right and wrong. In our daily lives, if we do not see the sun in the sky, it is not because the sun doesn't exist; it is because clouds cover it.

Every one of us has a different character as well as one's own understanding and power or ability to compromise. The ability to look through clouds and find the sun indicates common sense. Common sense allows one to compromise with another on the thoughts, beliefs, and knowledge to find common ground that better suits the overall human existence. History shows people who lived many, many years ago left their mark on society. Some individuals have created things, thereby making this world a better place to live. To do this, such individuals had to have an understanding of other people and things. There has to be reasoning to understand that at a certain point, we must come together at the midline. So, in other words, we have to have more in common than what separates us. This is a logical thing to follow but not easy to practice.

If people can compromise and find common ground, they can shake hands or perhaps even hug; they can become brothers or sisters. Our individual life in this world is brief because, in the grand scheme of civilization, fifty, sixty, or even ninety years are a small amount of time. If one were to ask someone what they have done during all those years, it would be very hard to recount all of their life's moments. There are people from different races and cultures. To achieve progress in life, people and cultures must understand and respect one another and compromise; in doing so, they accomplish advances for civilization. There have been great leaders throughout history, and many are still admired today. We render homage to these figures because, without their vision, we would have remained primitive. We salute those who invented electricity and all the advances it brought. We salute those who studied diseases and created preventative medicines and cures. Because of these individuals, our life span has increased. There are so many advances the human race has achieved. It would be ideal if a common understanding amongst people could achieve universal peace. This would bring tranquility to people, and this peaceful atmosphere would create advances and progress.

Looking back at history, there are those who stood out. History has put them on a pedestal, as in the case of Alexander the Great. Although he was a warrior and spread misery in the regions he invaded, he brought Greek civilization and its laws to the Persian Empire. He brought reasoning, freedom of expression and ideas and abolished a despotic system that existed at the time. All these changes had benefits. There were those that fought many wars, destroyed civilizations, and killed many people, as did Attila with his barbaric legions. What did they do for civilization? The answer is nothing, and their lack of understanding made them ignorant and arrogant. They would not follow advice and would not compromise. The only thing they followed was brute force. Their actions were like a hurricane that produced extermination and devastation. Nature produces those effects and consequences; people shouldn't.

If those human beings had the capacity to reason, all those bad things would not have happened or reached such an extreme. But again, the lack of reasoning was like those clouds in the sky that block the sun's rays. There were individuals like Stalin, Hitler, and Mussolini. They also caused much suffering and agony and created gross injustices, and I ask why. I cannot understand why those people did not see that everything they did caused so much destruction. What were they trying to accomplish? The suffering they caused turned one person against the other and shattered normal lives. Why this lack of comprehension and lack of communication? Because of their lack of understanding and arrogance, and being unwilling to compromise, they did not understand that everything is transient. They conquered areas that gave them temporary pleasure that didn't last, and that pleasure was based on other peoples' suffering. In other words, the minorities created injustice and subjugation of the majority. My question is, what would have happened if those injustices had been against the leaders? In all of these situations, if common sense was allowed to speak, perhaps many wars and much misery could have been avoided. I imagine that in such an environment, the happiness parents derive from seeing their children develop in a peaceful world would create future generations who will strive to live without hate and rancor.

I believe the world would be very different if logical reasoning and common sense prevailed. This would create respect, and the human race would flourish. Wars could be avoided and misery diminished. If the human race would follow this path, we could see the imaginary light written on the walls of old cities that would state: Here common sense prevails; each others' ideas are admired and protected, reasoning is appreciated, peace guides our lives, beauty adorns our daily lives, jails are empty for lack of clients. All those things would be ideal and are logical, but unfortunately, some don't see this as being logical. So, I ask myself, why is common sense not being applied? As human beings, we all have egos and strong opinions, and those opinions can be the clouds preventing us from seeing that sun we call common sense. There is no better way to understand each other and reason than to compromise with one another. Instead of insulting and degrading one another, we must learn to have common sense, talk, and find common ground.

In Donizetti's opera, *L'elisir d'amore*, there is Dr. Dulcamara, who sells a potion supposed to bring happiness. Instead, it brings misery to the poor soul who believes something unrealistic. This is because Dulcamara thinks of only his interests without thinking of the suffering and deceit his actions cause. Years and centuries pass, but the deceit and cunning of human beings do not. The beauty of life is not always appreciated, and certain souls have not seen the light. As Dante tells us in *The Inferno,* when these people are sentenced to the Inferno, in spite of everything, they will not repent and recognize their wrongdoings. In my opinion, the practical way of life is using common sense. It is not taking the elixir, which brings one fantasy and a temporary result. The elixir's effect dissipates when one removes the cork from the bottle and the alcohol evaporates; the poor person is deceived and humiliated. Like a fertile valley with water and sun, crops will grow and flourish. Likewise, tranquility, peace, and lack of war would enhance and favor invention, and the creation of things and peoples' lives would also flourish.

I believe parents have a responsibility to instill in their children's minds, from an early age, the ability to understand what is right and wrong, what is dangerous or not, and to have the ability to use common sense. Finding the right path for children to follow and using their thinking skills has been written about in so many stories. The ability to learn and use proper thinking skills will take and lead children through life with more understanding and clarity.

When a mother or father sends their child off into the world with all its dangers, it is not because the parent does not love the child; it is for the child to learn to be alert for that which can cause them to stray. An example of this would be a child being told years ago to fetch water for the family. This water was imperative for them to live. But, to get the water, the child had to walk through the forest. And, in this forest, there could be many dangers. The child who could sense danger and protect himself or flee from the danger succeeded in getting the water and returning that water to his family. If we, as parents, cannot teach our children these traits, how can we expect them to reject the elixir from those who want to hurt them and guide them down the wrong path? This is a huge responsibility, and sadly, many adults cannot live up to it. They are the ones who drink the elixir. To me, common sense is the most fundamental trait one can have as a human being to achieve our goals and survive. Without common sense, the species will self-destruct, and life will lose its meaning. Open the clouds, open your mind, use common sense, use reasoning, and you will then see the sun's rays.

Bringing a child into the world cannot be from a one-night of passion or inebriation. One has to assume responsibility for one's actions. In our world, too many of these events happen, and the by-product is born nine months later. Sometimes, this lack of planning can create an environment in which this child may go through life largely forging their own way. These babies have no defense and cry out in need for food and love. What will be if there is no family life and the adults who created this miracle are not responsible? Even in the animal kingdom, a mother usually defends her brood with her life, and the father forages for food. There is a sense of "family." Sadly, more often than I wish to hear about, this is not the case in today's world. Therefore, the lack of common sense is once again brought forth. The easy part of life is going out and having a good time. The hard part is assuming responsibility and taking accountability for one's actions.

Life is a beautiful thing; to be able to appreciate all the mystery around us, decipher the unknown and reach a conclusion is the miracle of interpretation and believing in something.

# Chapter 26
# Retired Life

After more than forty years of practice, the day arrived when I decided my strength was diminishing, and it seemed like my phone was ringing more often than before during the night, the emergencies more frequent, and the referring doctors who trusted me calling me more and more. This was a very difficult decision in my life and for my family. Emergencies took a lot of my time and mainly occurred during the night. After working all night, the following day, I still had to tend to the elective surgeries my office had scheduled. At some point, although surgery was my life and I loved what I did, my wife and I decided that it was time for me to retire.

Once I made this decision, as required, I sent out notifications to my patients. It was only then I realized how many people I had truly touched. Many of my former and current patients showed up crying. Others brought pastries, but all asked me the same question, "Why did I have to retire?" I let them know that after so many years, the energy and intensity of the practice were a lot for me. I wanted to spend time with my family and have enough time for myself to enjoy life after so many years of studying and then practicing. I referred them to other great doctors I trusted, and between hugs and tears, we said our goodbyes.

It was nostalgic but a necessary move on my part. Thank you to all my patients who were part of my life and for giving me the joy and pleasure of helping you. The trust you had in me meant everything. More chapters in my life needed to be written, and a new one was about to begin.

The week after I retired began with something I had been putting off for many years. I had surgery. Ever since I initially injured my left arm cleaning the gutters in my first home in Teaneck, I noticed the arm was never quite the same. As time passed, doing some surgical cases, primarily laparoscopic cases, I noticed I had limitations when holding the instruments with my left hand. Also, at that time, because Coco was getting older and could no longer fly, we would drive to Miami, and I noticed if I held the steering wheel with my left arm, I would have pain afterward when I lifted my arm. It reached a moment when I went to see a specialist, and he ordered a CAT scan. It showed I had a spur and some shredding of the tendon in that area. He recommended physical therapy which I did for six months, but my situation did not improve. I needed rotator cuff surgery. The recovery for this procedure would be at least five to six months because the tendon was torn, so it needed to be reattached and heal (you can't lift your arm above your shoulder). I was too busy in my practice with surgeries scheduled for months ahead and couldn't afford to take this length of time off. I continued my surgical practice and dealt with the pain for a few more years until retirement. I made an excellent recovery, and all is now well.

Once I had recovered, Roberta and I moved to North Miami to live in our beautiful condo at the Bella Mare on William's Island. Life was great. I finally had time to work out at my leisure, enjoy meals with my wife and soak in the beautiful views and a little sun here or there. I have never been one to sit in the sun too long because of its dangers to one's skin. As you know, I became sick there, so once again we moved. The move to The Villages wasn't ideal. I selected the wrong movers, and sadly, upon unpacking and seeing them unload our furniture, I noticed certain items were damaged, and Roberta was very unhappy. One damaged item was the concert piano belonging to Roberta's late father. Important items like these are sentimental, and seeing them damaged because of negligence and not being appropriately wrapped is very upsetting. Unfortunately, two beautiful chandeliers and a leather sofa were cracked and ruined. We went through the insurance, but sadly the damage was not fully covered.

Getting settled can take time: putting away all one's clothes, organizing the spice rack, and hanging artwork and electronics. A few months after moving to The Villages, Roberta and I headed up north for Vanessa's wedding. Right after Vanessa's wedding, when she was on her honeymoon, Roberta and I took the time to organize some of the 'extras' from our move from William's Island to The Villages. Vanessa had a rather large storage room in their house at the time, so we shipped some of our items up north to be stored there. It was a hot day in late May, and Roberta and I were busy going through and organizing everything. Not surprisingly, after reading this whole book and maybe knowing me a bit, you won't be surprised to hear I have been responsible during my life, and I have never smoked and drank only occasionally at social gatherings with friends.

While Roberta and I were diligently working, I became dizzy and stopped to rest. Roberta asked if I was OK, and of course, I said I was fine! Yes, I am the typical man: deny, deny. I resumed moving the boxes and small furniture items and again became dizzy. I had to sit down, and I knew something wasn't right. I went to see a former colleague who is also a friend and an Internist. My EKG (electrocardiogram) showed a very low heart rate of 40. This was not good. Coupled with my dizziness and a follow-up visit to the cardiologist, it was determined I needed another tune-up: I needed a pacemaker.

Vanessa returned from her honeymoon, and that evening, Roberta and I told her that I would be receiving a pacemaker the following day. Needless to say, she hadn't been anticipating this news or returning home to this. I arrived at the hospital the following morning and saw all my old friends and colleagues. Everyone was so wonderful and extra attentive; I felt like a king. The pacemaker went in without a hitch, and Vanessa and Roberta were waiting for me in my hospital room. I was recovering wonderfully and enjoying some time out in the Hamptons about ten days later when I received a call from Linda in Italy. My father had passed away.

Roberta immediately got me a ticket and packed my suitcase. For whatever reason, we had traveled north with our passports this time; otherwise, one of us would have had to fly to Florida first to get mine. Between my daughter's wedding, getting a pacemaker, and now my father's passing, all within less than a month, I was in shock. I arrived in Italy and saw so many relatives, friends of my father, and essentially the whole village. Those few days in Scauri were a mix of emotions. Each corner of the house awakened so many memories, emotions of the not-so-distant past, and the outdoor terrace where I sat with my mother. Those images and moments created a vast emptiness that took over me. I felt a tremendous solitude, like someone was removing my still-beating heart. I didn't see or hear from my brother during this time, so I dealt with the affairs on my own.

I stayed for a few weeks and had to clear out my parent's entire house because they left the house in Argentina to my brother; they left this house to me. I had no way to care for it from so far away, and frankly, it would be too sad to ever return without at least one of my parents occupying it, so I put it on the market with a neighbor and old friend of mine who still lives in Scauri. He wound up buying the property a few months later for himself. Trying to go over my father's affairs was awful. First of all, I have always been lucky and depended on Roberta, and to some extent Vanessa, as she became an adult and attorney, to deal with paperwork, etc., as it has never been my forte. Luckily, this same real estate broker and his daughter were able to help me sort through all my dad's old paperwork and pay any bills.

Coincidentally, my father was not the most organized with his paperwork. I remember all the years he would complain about having just come back on the bus from Formia, having gone there to dispute a payment. Even in his old age, he would travel there with whatever receipts he kept or could find to dispute a second charge or interest for something when the company for the water or garbage collection hadn't received a payment. My father had quite a temper, and at his advanced age, he would become easily aggravated and end up paying again. He was enraged about the injustice and people taking advantage of him, especially at his age, when he couldn't locate specific receipts from several years back.

On my last day there, before returning home, I was walking, and for whatever reason, I stopped. I began to admire the structure of the house my father once built with his hands. Its balcony. The many pots for different flowers and how, at one time, he maintained everything so perfectly and pristinely. He grew tomatoes, grapes, green beans, and parsley; you name it, he would grow it. As the years passed and his movements became restricted, I thought of how he would clamber up the stairs with his cane while pulling on the handrail. I know all the freshness of everything contributed to both of my parents' long lives.

What I saw now was a sad memory of those days when the house was bright, and the windows and doors were open. There was life in the house with my parents, family, and their friends. Where there were once paintings on the walls were now just old walls with some scratches and stains, and the doors and windows were closed and dark. I left very early in the morning, and at 4 A.M., I was waiting at the local station to take the train to Rome. I was tired and thought perhaps I would never see this place again. I have distant cousins who remain in Italy, and Vanessa's godfather, to this day, lives next door to where my parents did. Whenever I speak with any of these people, they always ask when Roberta and I will be coming to visit. My answer is always the same; I can't visit because the main attraction isn't there. It's like having a Ferrari without gas in the desert. I prefer to keep the memories as they were, alive.

It's a fact of life and something my former profession reminds me of every day but like an unrealistic person, for a son to accept this cruel destiny is never easy.

# Chapter 27
# The Economic Collapse of 2008

As you know, my wife and I have enjoyed some real estate transactions during our years. The financial crisis of 2007-2008, arguably the largest financial crisis since the Great Depression, affected almost everyone. Roberta and I saw our investment portfolio take a tremendous dive, and even though it's paper money, in the sense that you never held or realized the gains, to see such a sharp decrease in numbers is never easy. I should say that during the course of writing this book, the Coronavirus has also wreaked havoc on the global economy.

I decided at this time that Vanessa should move out of our apartment in NYC, and we would rent out the condominium. Vanessa was dating and spending more and more time out in NJ, and the timing of everything dictated that this made sense. So we listed the apartment for rent. In the interim, I should mention that Vanessa has always loved the easternmost beaches of Long Island, otherwise known as the Hamptons, and for over the last two decades had said that Roberta and I should invest there. In fact, Vanessa had been enjoying summers out there for about twelve years at this juncture and had become very familiar with the real estate market. Then, around 2009, she again brought up this investment opportunity since the market crisis had very much impacted the largely second-home market out there, and many homes were available for much less than they were valued at or the price they were listed for a year or two before.

Vanessa and I took several trips out to the Hamptons, and we found a short sale available for less than half of the home's original asking price. The house was small, old and falling apart, but the property and location were beautiful. The existing owners had put in a pool and a small pool house and cottage. I knew this would be a great opportunity for Vanessa, as she could rebuild this home over time and rent it in the interim. I was very happy to help Vanessa start her future. The summer rental market in the Hamptons is quite something! The closing occurred several months later, and Vanessa embarked on some immediate repairs to the small home. She finished the basement and expanded its tiny kitchen, and I have to say she did a lovely job. The house was rented for the whole season the very first summer she listed it.

As the years passed, it became apparent that the house needed to be torn down and rebuilt. It was extremely energy inefficient, and its decks were falling apart. In addition, the bedrooms were on the main floor with the kitchen and living room upstairs, and one had to go down the old stairs to use the bathroom. After much deliberation, we all decided it would be best to tear down the existing structure, move the home's location slightly and pour a new foundation. Little did we realize the scope of the project we were embarking upon. It took ten months alone to obtain the necessary building permits! Between the time we submitted our initial permit application and before its approval, the building codes were changed, and our plans needed to be updated to adhere to new environmental conservation and electrical mandates. This should have been a sign of what was to come.

As I mentioned, although the main structure on the property was old, the home was purchased with a new pool and two small cottages on the property. The former owners had taken a second home loan for this construction project, and when the financial markets collapsed, they could not continue paying on both this and the original mortgage loan; hence the property wound up in a short-sale situation. Vanessa never touched the pool or cottages. Before the building permit was granted, some paperwork was needed to clarify the legality of the pool and cottages; this was provided, and the permits were granted.

We demolished the existing structure in October of 2015, and a new big hole was dug for the new home's foundation. The foundation was poured and construction began. Like most construction, the initial time estimates were far surpassed. Lennon was two at the time and attended school only twice a week. In order to keep things moving along and for Vanessa to be present on the weekends, Roberta, Vanessa, Lennon, and I would drive out every Tuesday and return every Friday to supervise the construction and make any immediate decisions or deal with any new issues. Because the house had no heat or running water at this point, we stayed in the small cottage. The first few weeks, the cottage didn't have heat either, and being February, it was very cold. We brought a space heater, heavy clothes, and lots of blankets and made do. In some ways, it was a lot of fun and a close time together. We used the barbecue to make our meals and would watch TV together as Lennon made her way around the small space.

Before passing inspection, in the months between February and August of 2018, we dealt with a whole host of problems, including having to re-vegetate two hundred and fifty square feet of property with hundreds of specific plants and shrubs, yet another legal issue with the existing cottages which had not been touched, as well as a health department issue of an existing water line under the untouched cottages. Although I could type this in one paragraph, the months of back and forth for these items, the cost, stress, and headaches convinced Roberta and Vanessa that the project would never end and was a money pit.

My 42nd wedding anniversary was August the 8th, 2018, and we began the day remembering our young days and when we started to date. The home was finally finished, and it was a beautiful Hampton summer day. I was admiring the beautiful home we were able to build for our daughter and her family while hearing the sweet, little voice of my granddaughter playing. On this day, our builder arrived to announce our home finally, finally passed inspection! We were over the moon with relief and overjoyed that our lives could at last move on, and Vanessa could now begin to use and, more importantly, rent this home. Oddly enough, with every triumph comes a tragedy because that very day, we received news that my cousin, Peter, had passed away. Uncle Peter was eighty-five years old.

Peter, or in Italian, Pietro, was the husband of my Aunt Giuseppina's second child and oldest daughter, Edda. Pietro came to the United States and was a mechanic. He was a very strong, tall man who commanded a presence in any room. His energy was infectious, and we all adored him. I used to enjoy speaking with him at our family gatherings, and we would discuss soccer and our lives. Vanessa always had a very special spot for her Uncle Peter as well. He was just that type of person. When Peter was in his early eighties, he was diagnosed with Parkinson's disease, which as anyone with experience knows, is a crippling and sad disease. As the disease progressed, Peter became confined to a wheelchair, and his spirit slowly left him, and his infectious smile became more of a rigid expression. Roberta and I were lucky enough to have visited Peter just two weeks before his passing. I often think of him and hope he is at peace.

# Chapter 28
# The Villages

It was a very quick decision to move to The Villages, both in purchasing the home there and how quickly our apartment on William's Island sold. Roberta, not being as in love with The Villages as I was, began questioning our rashness in purchasing the home. I understood this, but in my mind, not all or even some surgeries are the same, and sometimes, quite often, in fact, split-second decisions have to be made that can determine whether a patient lives or dies. Faulty or not, I often apply this to my daily life. Roberta has slowly come to appreciate some aspects of The Villages. We have some lovely friends and continue to expand upon our memories here. Shortly after my return from Italy, Vanessa shared the great news that she was expecting.

Lennon was born and joined their already full family of four children. This past Christmas, everyone came to visit and stay with us in The Villages. We had continual daily excitement, and there were toys spread out all over the entire house, along with the sounds of various Ipads playing at different volumes. At my age, I won't lie; sometimes, this can produce a sense of anxiety for me. With all the activity going on, I sit on the sofa, and to some extent, I am part of all that action – in a passive state. Those few days when we were all together were like good medicine for our souls, and Lennon's constant running kept us all active. However, I can't take credit away from Roberta, as it's her nature to be part of Lennon's games, running back and forth and making sure she was enjoying herself. The days spent together were beautiful, but unfortunately, the day came when we had to say goodbye. I became nostalgic, and that feeling made me aware of the house's emptiness all of a sudden. It was like a deprived life because the noises and the running around were just memories. Thankfully technology has given us the telephone and video calls because the distance seems less. The fact that we can see their faces and hear their voices reactivates the memories of those days, and I hope in the future, we will have many, many more.

Roberta and I rent a small apartment in the next town from Vanessa. Roberta goes back and forth every few weeks because she needs her fix of Vanessa and Lennon. I read, cook outside on my lanai and do things; like installing a Ring doorbell system to occupy my time. I have also been busy writing this book!

Retirement has had a lot more excitement than I ever imagined, in all ways. I took up golf at the age of seventy-six. I play once or twice a week with a group of my guy friends. The Villages is huge and has over sixty golf courses I can bounce between. I drive a golf cart most places and have taken up biking to some extent. Sometimes Roberta and I go to the town square and listen to music or dine out at a restaurant alone or with our new friends. I feel relaxed in my environment here, something I never had in all the years I was struggling and then working; always anxious for that sense of contentment I now have. *La vita e'belle* (Life is beautiful)!

CONVERSATIONS WITH ROBERT: Since the first day I discovered and visited The Villages, I fell in love with the place and the type of life I am able to enjoy here. During any given week, there are more than two thousand, yes, that's right, two THOUSAND activities one can choose to participate in or attend. There are different town squares, each with live music and dancing in the evenings. I like to do my own thing during the day, which often is to ride my bike along the many different golf cart paths that follow along all the roads; these paths are used by walkers, runners, cyclists, and golf carts. They run for miles and miles, and you can spend hours and hours following various routes. The paths are all perfectly maintained and highlighted by meticulously planted gardens adorned by sculpted palm trees and colorful plants and flowers. The flowers and the colorful insects and butterflies they attract all seem so peaccful and harmonious to me. Because of this, I can easily walk or bike many miles, enjoying my music and taking in the landscape. Sometimes, I listen to lectures about various topics like history or debates about current world topics affecting so much of this country and the world.

At some point, my body lets me know it's time to pause and rest for a few minutes. Perhaps, not surprisingly, I have a routine and stop at one particular bench to hydrate and catch up with my friend, Robert, who has never missed one of our morning meetings. Robert is someone who perhaps used to travel the same paths I do, and according to the family label present on the back of the bench I rest on, he was only a few years older than me when he passed away. It seems he was a nice guy and is missed based on the words written on this plaque. In my own time, I started to befriend Robert and have conversations with him in my thoughts. After I salute him and inquire how it's going, I wonder what he is doing and how things are on the other side; as we here don't know, and there always seems to be a lot of confusion about the afterlife and heaven. It's like how the Tower of Babel confused people and made them unable to understand one another; perhaps this modified our DNA somehow, which is why we don't have a clear picture of how heaven is or what transpires over there.

I have an inquisitive mind, and there remain receptors in my brain, despite my different experiences in life, that have never been used, and perhaps they want to make history in some way. They say one will never know, but at this point, I feel confident that Robert wants his solitude; I understand that and respect his desire. As such, I bid my goodbyes and promise to return the next day, only whispering to him not to forget and let me know how he is doing, and perhaps one day, when the time comes, I will have the opportunity to meet him. I am not in a rush, however, and I still enjoy finding nice, good human beings on this Earth for now.

One day I was listening to a beautiful opera by Christoph Gluck called *Orfeo ed Euridice*. This opera was composed in 1762 and is still well-received today. The tender, sweet music tells a story of ancient times when life was simple and natural in this bucolic place where shepherds, animals, rivers, and birds all seem to enjoy the moment and occasion. The happiest of all was Euridice; a young girl, full of life, who was very happy because that day she was going to marry her sweetheart, Orfeo, and in preparation for such a joyful occasion, she was gathering fresh flowers in the field to make herself a crown for the special day of her wedding. The young girls were going from one place to another, laughing and teasing each other with the motion of bending their bodies to pick the flowers with their long hair falling and obstructing their view. Very graciously, with one hand, Euridice set her hair in place, and with the other hand, she selected the best flowers. All was harmonious and joyful until suddenly, the calm was interrupted when Euridice screamed with a loud, painful cry. Euridice had failed to notice a serpent nesting between some flowers, and she was bitten on the hand. The pain was intense, her skin color was fading, and the happiness and joy present just a few minutes ago was no longer heard or visible. Sadly, her loud cry for help was heard, but unfortunately, it was too late. Orfeo was made aware of his loss, and his laments were so powerful that even the god, Amore, was moved to compassion and granted Orfeo his wish to bring back Euridice. I think of and tell this story because, at one point, Orfeo asks Euridice to respond to his laments and says, "Tu non rispondi." (You are not answering me.) I can't help but wonder why Robert doesn't respond to my requests either.

I wish my friend Robert a nice day and proceed with my bicycling, saluting some friendly faces along the way. Sometimes I stop and chat with these folks after seeing them a few times; obviously, I am not short of words or time to share them these days. It's amazing how many people are interested in finding out I have an accent! After all these years, my accent has followed me like a shadow. This shadow saw me from the beginning all the way until now. So now, to me, he is really a true friend, someone always there, not just during the good times of my life. He was able to see me through some very dark times, and for this, I respect him like a solid companion who sticks with you, and I know he will continue doing this until the end. I acknowledge that, yes, I have an accent and give them a brief summation of my history which you already know. We exchange some opinions and interests, and after a while, I depart, stopping at the area where I pick up my mail. Because each neighborhood has a mail area close to its residences, I almost always find a neighbor or two there and engage in some light chitchat as I gather my mail.

Once I arrive home, if it's a nice, warm day, I hop into the pool and do some light exercise, followed by a refreshing shower. This is how my days go. I look forward to each day till the next time when I will visit my friend Robert in the delight of thinking maybe he will have some news for me and an answer to my question. As the saying goes, one never knows. There is  beauty in not knowing the future of our lives, even though we all would love to see the future

# Chapter 29
# Lucky Guy

Considering my life with all of its circumstances and the things I encountered, I can say I am a lucky guy. I was born during a war into a world of uncertainty. The young men of the time were off fighting, leaving the elderly to care for themselves and young women to try to protect their children. Children like me were born without prenatal care, and women, like my mother, were generally helped as best as they could be during labor by other women, as there were few or no doctors and no access to a hospital.

As you know, when I was a child, I sustained a laceration of the forehead during a bombing. I was lucky because the injuries could have been much worse. I could have been blinded or killed. If either of those things had happened, I would not be here sharing my story with you.

I am a lucky guy because I grew up with my mother and father, who weren't killed during the war. Many other children of the time were left to grow up motherless or fatherless or, even worse, as an orphan.

I am lucky because I had parents and elders who encouraged, supported, and guided me towards seeking a different path than their own. They fought for and believed in me despite the period in which I was fighting my circumstances and desperation, and I could not see the light at the end of the tunnel. Not everyone is fortunate to have this. Others may have materialistic benefits; however, this doesn't mean they are taught or experience the real meaning of life.

I am a lucky guy because destiny gave me the opportunity to find and marry a remarkable woman as an inseparable companion, who, in my more difficult days, cried without me even noticing her tears.

I am a lucky guy because I was blessed with the birth of a daughter who has been the pride of my life and then gave me my granddaughter, Lennon, who now I watch with pride as she grows and develops into her own person.

I am a lucky guy because I wasn't infected with a disease when I punctured myself with a needle. My young friend died in this very situation, and I was so fortunate this was never my destiny. I guess it just wasn't my time.

I am lucky because I live in and have been able to raise my daughter in a country where there is not a system of socialized medicine. This will never better or even remotely match the current medical system in the United States, even with its faults.

I am a lucky guy because, on June 29, 1983, a portion of the bridge on Route I95 in Connecticut collapsed, causing several fatalities. Less than seventy-two hours prior, Roberta and I crossed that bridge with Vanessa, who was only three years old at the time. We were returning from my cousins' house and were fortunate to make it home safely.

I am a lucky guy because the train of my life was going at such a high rate of speed I was forced to wear blinders, but now that the train has slowed down, I can appreciate the panoramic view and see things I was not able to see before.

I am a lucky guy for thousands of reasons. Being a surgeon, I saw a great deal of suffering and sadness. However, at the same time, I was able to help these people. In my forty years of practice, I saved many lives and gave hope to many others.

I am a lucky guy because, despite so much adversity, I could move past it. I was able to forge through it all and realized I could succeed, and kept moving forward. I faced many uncertainties and much sadness, but ultimately, I prevailed, and this was because

I kept going. One never knows what is possible, and to me, even more so in this land of America because to me, this is the promised Land.

I will consider myself a lucky guy if this book is a source of inspiration and hope to others. I hope to give others motivation to move ahead no matter what stumbling blocks they face. Aspire to move ahead regardless of what others say to discourage you. Move ahead because of your dreams. Hope is never giving up. Be persistent, and you will arrive at your destination. It may not be tomorrow, but you will arrive.

# Epilogue

This is the story of my life. Like almost all human beings, I have had my ups and downs. The beginnings of my life were very difficult and, at times, unbearable. However, I was always loved, and this was a huge asset. I was fortunate to grow up in a stable home environment despite the outside world being unstable and our finances being meager. Seeing how much this country offers to its youth in terms of education and awareness, I know my undergraduate schooling lacked proper guidance and offered limited opportunities.

My parents were very simple people who tried in their own way to do the best they could. They instilled certain values in me, and because of that, I could distinguish right from wrong and do the right thing. Unfortunately, like any human, I was not always correct in my decisions. However, I feel my upbringing prevented me from making majorly regrettable decisions that could have potentially compromised my future in any serious way.

I compare my life to a small seed blowing in the wind and landing on a large rock with a porous surface. The seed lodges in one of the crevices, planting its roots. To the average observer, this plant's chance of survival and growing strong may seem limited, but with the space available, given sunlight and rain, the plant will naturally do anything possible to adhere its roots firmly in the dirt and reach toward the sun. I was a seed looking for a place to plant my roots. I was at the mercy of the wind and weather, being blown about and in all different directions.

I am eternally grateful for my parents, who, in their very limited way, stimulated my curiosity about things they had limited knowledge of. I am thankful to my close and distant family for always supporting and believing in me. It is because of them I never truly lost hope. I am indebted to this beautiful country that offered me the opportunity of a future. I am convinced there is no other place on earth like this land...GOD BLESS AMERICA.

END OF MY ODYSSEY: I mentioned how the idea of this book came about. It started with someone hearing my stories and seeing their potential. The facts were there, but it took a few people with the knowledge and art of recognizing that potential, which is not common.

When Michelangelo completed the statue of David, its beauty, proportions, and perfect anatomical display, amazed people. There were few who knew the large piece of marble Michelangelo used was one that had been exposed to inclement weather for years in the Medici back yard. When Michelangelo was asked how he made this incredible work of art, he simply stated. "David was there all the time, and I just had to bring him out."

I remember not knowing about multiple-choice questions, and when I asked how they worked, I was told the answers were listed below each question. Faced with the extensive size of the Roman Empire and continuous revolts, Diocletian, the Roman Emperor from 284 to 305, divided the empire into two parts. He remained to govern the east end of the Empire, and Maximian governed the west. At some point, Diocletian decided he'd had enough and wanted a simple life. He abdicated the throne and forced Maximian to leave the throne as well. Diocletian retired to his beautiful palace in Salone, in the Dalmatia region, where he enjoyed caring for his garden. Maximian continued to write to Diocletian, insisting they should return to their reign, to which Diocletian's response was simple.... "You should see how beautiful my vegetables are."

One day when I was with a group of friends and talking to this one lady, upon hearing a little bit of my story and being intrigued by my foreign accent, she saw potential that, unbeknown to me, I was not able to appreciate. It is my life story, but because it was too close to me, I could not see its potential. During our lives on this earth, we, in one way or another, leave our mark in very different forms, like the footprints of people running from danger thousands of years ago. Those footprints are like pictures we take, so in the future, we can look back and remember with nostalgia the days when we were young and full of energy. Sometimes those days remind us of being ready to climb the mountain of life, but perhaps we didn't have the right equipment or shoes at the time to face the harsh weather at the summit. The irony is that so many years later when one can usually better afford the proper equipment, their only option is to look at the mountain because the physical ability to climb it is no longer there.

I love my family because my wife was able to balance my weaknesses with my extreme desire to succeed and knew that given the opportunity, I would prevail. We both knew it would take some time for this to happen, but I knew it would because my mother once told me the sun would shine for me too. Because of my faith and belief in her, I can tell you that I have arrived after a long journey. Like Odysseus, after ten years of searching for his home and wishing to see his wife, Penelope, and his son, Telemachus, I am lucky to be home, to enjoy my dear family, and appreciate my good fortune. I am tremendously appreciative of this country for giving me the many opportunities it has, and I thank God for even when my small boat was facing the storm, and all seemed like it would capsize and end up at the bottom of the sea, for allowing my inner voice to tell me not to despair because your time has not come yet; you still have a long way to go. I am grateful for all of this.

My granddaughter will be five years old this May, and this book was written with her and her future in mind. There are so many questions in my head, and I don't have the answers to all of them because I am not able to read the future. I don't have the assurances of Aeneas, who, after living in Troy, went to Italy to the city of Cuma, where he was able to speak to the Sybil to inquire about his future and was assured of a great future for him and his family. Us mortals don't get such assurances. I am grateful. I think I am a lucky guy.

GENERAL NOTE: I am not an expert on the problems of the world, its economic conditions, politics, or religion. My training and specialty involved medicine, a totally different field. When I mentioned other topics throughout the book, I did so to clarify or sharpen the points I was trying to make. I hope I have accomplished this in an open and respectful manner. Sometimes, when uncovering ashes that seem to be dead, with just a little oxygen, that flame can be reactivated after lying dormant, but not wholly extinguished, for so long. This is like one continuing to fight for their life so their story and experience can live on.

I wrote this book with many ideas, stories, and occasional quotes from operas and classic authors. I want, in some way, for my readers to be stimulated, not for the action, and hopefully, you will find some, but so there is a curiosity for knowledge of the past. After all, look at the advances gained from Columbus, the Pasteurs, and Leonardo da Vinci. We enjoy these advances daily, and mostly, I tried to briefly describe each of my historical or literary acknowledgments, hoping it would inspire each of you to further inquire about something, do some homework and find me to tell me more about it.

This book started like a small, gradually germinating seed. It started with my wife and daughter constantly urging me to make a journal for Lennon, something to bring her light on her dark days so she could always know her roots. With time, I realized this is not something I should take lightly or be indifferent to. Like anything in life, a tipping point is reached, and the more I wrote and became entrenched in my chapters, the more I became interested in sharing my story, my ups and downs, and reliving the days of my past. During certain chapters, I became very emotional. Several times I had to stop writing because the tears blurred my vision, like those first few days as a young boy when I was separated from my parents to attend the Jovenado.

I think the beauty of the unpredictability of life is precious. Not knowing what the future has in store for us takes away our predestination because if one knows our future is doomed, no one would fight or waste time. However, there can always be more past the doom if one tries hard enough and doesn't give up. Looking back, if I had to do it all over again, the best lesson I learned would be to find and see a logical application in something for the future. I would ask many more questions in order to find the right direction faster, without so much back and forward that only wasted my time and energy. Because of my uncertainty and insecurity, I didn't pursue English at a younger age, and I should have, even knowing I might never need it.

Again, going back to the environment that surrounded me, I was like a small flower choked by taller grass. I will never stop thanking God for allowing me even to contemplate the possibility of scaling the many mountains before me. Just looking at those mountains would make you think it was an impossible achievement. Even more so, I knew that even if I could somehow do this, no one would be waiting for me on the other side, cheering me on. You feel alone, and that is a terrible feeling to have. It's important to remember you always have yourself and God. Never give up on yourself and your dreams. Fight for them, and don't lose hope. "Do not go gentle into that good night. Rage, rage against the dying of the light." — Dylan Thomas

# HISTRIA
## BOOKS

GAUDIUM

# GAUDIUM PUBLISHING
## BOOKS TO CHALLENGE AND ENLIGHTEN

OLIVIA GOODREAU

## BUT SHE LOOKS FINE
### FROM ILLNESS TO ACTIVISM

## NETWORKS RISING
THINKING TOGETHER IN A FLATTER WORLD

CHRISTOPHER BURNS

DOUG GRECO

## TO FIND A KILLER.
### THE HOMOPHOBIC MURDERS OF NORMA AND MARIA HURDATO

Firas Jumaah and Charlotta Turner

## RESCUED FROM ISIS
## TERROR
How a University Professor Organized a Commando Mission to Rescue Her Doctoral Student from Isis-Controlled Iraq

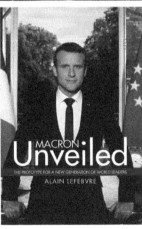

## MACRON Unveiled
THE PROTOTYPE FOR A NEW GENERATION OF WORLD LEADERS
ALAIN LEFEBVRE

## THE DOWNFALL
NIKLAS HAGEBACK
OF CHINA OR CCP 3.0